Thinking
and Acting
Like a

D1604689

Cognitive
School
Counselor

*For Jonathan, Drew, and Kristian . . . Three men whom
I love dearly and am so very proud to call my sons.*

RICHARD D. PARSONS

Thinking and Acting Like a Cognitive School Counselor

CORWIN
A SAGE Company

For information:

Corwin
A SAGE Company
2455 Teller Road
Thousand Oaks, California 91320
(800) 233-9936
Fax: (800) 417-2466
www.corwinpress.com

SAGE Ltd.
1 Oliver's Yard
55 City Road
London EC1Y 1SP
United Kingdom

SAGE India Pvt. Ltd.
B 1/I 1 Mohan Cooperative
    Industrial Area
Mathura Road, New Delhi 110 044
India

SAGE Asia-Pacific Pte. Ltd.
33 Pekin Street #02-01
Far East Square
Singapore 048763

Printed in the United States of America.

Library of Congress Cataloging-in-Publication Data

Parsons, Richard D.
Thinking and acting like a cognitive school counselor / Richard D. Parsons.
    p. cm.
Includes bibliographical references and index.
ISBN 978-1-4129-6648-1 (cloth)
ISBN 978-1-4129-6649-8 (pbk.)
    1. Educational counseling—Vocational guidance. 2. Cognitive styles. I. Title.

LB1027.5.P3195 2009
371.4—dc22   2009010943

This book is printed on acid-free paper.

09   10   11   12   13   10   9   8   7   6   5   4   3   2   1

Acquisitions Editor:	Arnis Burvikovs
Associate Editor:	Desirée A. Bartlett
Production Editor:	Eric Garner
Copy Editor:	Gretchen Treadwell
Typesetter:	C&M Digitals (P) Ltd.
Proofreader:	Carole Quandt
Indexer:	Judy Hunt
Cover Designer:	Michael Dubowe

Contents

Preface

School Counseling From a Cognitive Perspective

The issues confronted by today's school counselor demand rapid, effective resolution. Research on the use of cognitive strategies and techniques with school-aged children makes a compelling argument for school counselors' counseling from a cognitive perspective (e.g., Kendall, Gosch, Furr, & Sood, 2008; Choate-Summers et al., 2008).

Counseling from a cognitive perspective certainly sounds appropriate for a school setting. And, it is! In the pages that follow, you will be introduced or perhaps reintroduced to the fundamental principles underlying counseling from a cognitive perspective. The descriptions and illustrations will point to strategies to use with your students in the creation of "therapeutic" cognitive dissonance and the reeducation process needed to facilitate their development of adaptive beliefs and responses. But, the fundamental principles, techniques, and intervention strategies employed by a school counselor operating from a cognitive perspective are only part of the focus of this text.

More than sixty years ago, Pepinsky and Pepinsky (1954) recognized that if counseling is considered, in part, a cognitive activity, then the process of becoming a counselor must involve the acquisition of cognitive skills, and not just behavioral skills of social interaction. However, it is not unusual to find school counselors who have gone through training programs that provided extensive training in theory, research, and relationship building but very little guidance or training on how to translate these theoretical concepts and empirical findings into *practice*.

For those in training and those recently graduated, encounters with "real clients" are most often accompanied by apprehension and anxiety about knowing *what to do* and *when to do it.* It is an apprehension that is the hallmark of the novice counselor and one that distinguishes novice from expert. Understanding the theory is insufficient. The practicing counselor must translate theory into specific, action-oriented steps that will help to discern relevant client information and then formulate and implement effective intervention strategies.

Thinking and Acting Like a Cognitive School Counselor addresses this need to help counselors learn to, first, think like the experts and, then, *act* accordingly. The unique value of *Thinking and Acting Like a Cognitive School Counselor* is that it goes beyond the presentation of a theory and assists the reader to step into that theory, embrace it as an organizational framework, and then—and most importantly—employ it to guide their procedural thinking when confronted with client information.

TEXT FORMAT AND CHAPTER STRUCTURE

The book will be organized around the following parts. In Part I, the reader is introduced to a reflective-practitioner model of school counseling (Chapter 1) and the fundamentals of a cognitive orientation (Chapter 2). With these serving as a foundation, Part II identifies specific therapeutic targets and strategies that can be used to reach each target. Chapter 3 discusses strategies for assisting students to understand and "own" the connection of thoughts to feelings. Chapter 4 presents strategies to employ in helping the student discern functional from dysfunctional cognitions. Chapter 5, the final chapter of this section, presents strategies that will assist in the reeducation process and facilitate the student's development of more adaptive and functional ways of viewing him- or herself and the world, thus affecting change in both emotional and behavioral reactions. The final part of the book, Part III, invites the reader to first "observe" the thinking of a school counselor operating from a cognitive-orienting framework (Chapter 6), and then to actually apply this orientation to case materials (Chapter 7).

Research suggests that procedural knowledge—that is, knowing what to do when the student does this or that—is acquired as the result of practice accompanied by feedback. As such, *practice and feedback are central to this text.* Case illustrations, and case presentations with analyses of counselor actions and the decision-making processes underlying them, along with guided-practice activities, will be employed as "teaching tools" throughout the text.

As with all texts of this nature, this book is but a beginning. For school counselors embracing the value and efficacy of a cognitive framework to guide their reflections "on" and "in" their practice, additional training, supervision and professional development is a must. Hopefully, *Thinking and Acting Like a Cognitive School Counselor* provides a good springboard to that end.

—RDP

Acknowledgments

While I have been credited with the authorship of this text, many others have significantly contributed to the formation and shaping of my thoughts into the text you hold in your hands. First, I want to thank Arnis Burvikovs at Corwin for encouraging me to pursue this book series. I would like to acknowledge the support and encouragement I have received from my colleagues, particularly Naijian Zhang, Wally Kahn, and Charles Good. I sincerely appreciate the hard work and editorial support provided me by my graduate assistant, Erica Morrison, as well as the fine work of Gretchen Treadwell. Finally, I would like to publicly thank my wife, Ginny, not only for her professional insights but also for ongoing affirmation and support.

—RDP

Corwin gratefully acknowledges the contributions of the following individuals:

Cynthia Knowles, Prevention Specialist
Livonia Central School District
Livonia, NY

Katy Olweiler, Counselor
Lakeside School
Seattle, WA

Diane Smith, School Counselor
Smethport Area School District
Smethport, PA

Joyce Stout, Elementary School Counselor
Redondo Beach Unified School District
Redondo Beach, CA

Kay Herting Wahl, Director of School Counseling
Clinical Training Director
University of Minnesota
Minneapolis, MN

About the Author

© 2008 John Shetron

Richard D. Parsons, PhD, is a full professor in the Department of Counseling and Educational Psychology at West Chester University in Eastern Pennsylvania. Dr. Parsons has over thirty-two years of university teaching in counselor preparation programs. Prior to his university teaching, Dr. Parsons spent nine years as a school counselor in an inner-city high school. Dr. Parsons has been the recipient of many awards and honors, including the Pennsylvania Counselor of the Year award.

Dr. Parsons has authored or coauthored over eighty professional articles and books. His most recent books include the texts: *Counseling Strategies That Work! Evidenced-Based for School Counselors* (2006), *The School Counselor as Consultant* (2004), *Teacher as Reflective Practitioner and Action Researcher* (2001), *Educational Psychology* (2001), *The Ethics of Professional Practice* (2000), *Counseling Strategies and Intervention Techniques* (1994), and *The Skills of Helping* (1995). In addition to these texts, Dr. Parsons has authored or coauthored three seminal works in the area of psycho-educational consultation, *Mental Health Consultation in the Schools* (1993), *Developing Consultation Skills* (1985), and *The Skilled Consultant* (1995).

Dr. Parsons has a private practice and serves as a consultant to educational institutions and mental health service organizations throughout the tri-state area. Dr. Parsons has served as a national consultant to the Council of Independent Colleges in Washington, DC, providing institutions of higher education with assistance in the areas of program development, student support services, pedagogical innovation and assessment procedures.

Introduction
to Book Series

Transforming Theory Into Practice

There was a time—at least this is what I've been told—when school counselors were called upon to calm the child who lost his lunch, intervene with two middle school students who were "name-calling," and provide guidance to a senior considering college options. Now, I know these tasks are still on school counselors' "things-to-do lists," but a brief review of any one typical day in the life of a school counselor will suggest that these were the good old days!

You do not need the research or statistics on divorce rates, violence, drug use, sexual abuse, etc. to "know" that our society and our children are in crises. Each of the multitude of referrals you receive provides you with abundant evidence of this crisis.

It is not just the increased number of children seeking your assistance that is the issue—it is the increased severity and complexity of problems with which they present. The problems addressed by today's school counselor certainly include "name calling" and teasing, but sadly, in today's society, that form of interaction can quickly escalate to violence involving deadly weapons. Perhaps you still have the child or two who is upset about misplaced lunches—or homework, or jackets—but it is also not unusual to find the upset is grounded in the anticipated abuse that will be received when his or her parent finds out.

School children with significant depression, debilitating anxieties, energy-draining obsessions, damaged self-concepts, and self-destructive behaviors can be found in any school and in any counselor's office throughout our land. Responding to these children in ways that facilitate their development and foster their growth through education is a daunting task for today's school counselor. It is a task that demands a high degree of knowledge, skill, and competency. It is a task that demands effective, efficient translation of theory and research into practice.

The current series, *Transforming Theory Into Practice*, provides school counselors practical guides to gathering and processing client data, developing case conceptualizations, and formulating and implementing specific treatment plans. Each book in the series emphasizes skill development and, as such, each book provides extensive case illustrations and guided-practice exercises in order to move the reader from simply "knowing" to "doing."

The expanding needs of our children, along with the demands for increased accountability in our profession, require that each of us continue to sharpen our knowledge and skills as helping professionals. It is the hope that the books presented within this series, *Transforming Theory Into Practice*, facilitate your own professional development and support you in your valued work of counseling our children.

Part I

Using a Cognitive Orientation to Guide Reflection

Using a cognitive orientation to guide reflection, while intellectually interesting, remains just theory until it is translated into practice. The process of gathering student information, discerning what is important from what is not, and knowing what needs to be done to move the student from the "what is" to the "what is desired" requires more than knowledge of theory or the blind application of technique.

In Part I, the fundamental principles of a cognitive approach will be presented as a valuable, orienting framework to be used by the school counselor as he or she develops case conceptualization and treatment plans. In Chapter 1, the reader will be introduced to the concept and value of reflective practice. In essence, reflective practice is the ability of the counselor to think about a case before contact, after a session, and while in interaction with the student and to use the insights gained from such reflection to develop and adjust effective treatment plans. Reflective practice demands the counselors use of an orienting framework in order to make sense out of the student's disclosures and allow those to give shape to the counselor's response. As such, the guiding philosophy and principles underlying the specific strategies and techniques of cognitive therapy/counseling are presented in Chapter 2.

The School Counselor as Reflective Practitioner

1

Noting that Charles is upset and angry about something is certainly stating the obvious. However, what may be less apparent is the source of this anger and the steps needed to not only reduce the anger and perhaps resolve the situation, but also to empower Charles in such a way to prevent the likelihood of such anger being experienced again.

Perhaps as your read the above quote from Charles, you began to generate a number of "hypotheses" about what may be going on, as well as what you, as counselor, would need to do. While trained to be good listeners, school counselors understand that listening is but the vehicle to understanding and that understanding is the base from which we formulate our helping strategies.

COUNSELORS IN SEARCH OF MEANING

Charles's declaration is actually an invitation to the counselor to engage in a process of reflection and search for meaning. This reflective process is one of discernment. It is a process through which the school counselor discerns what is important from what is not, understands the "what is" opposed to "what is hoped for," and develops connections that will guide the student to this desired outcome.

For example, the counselor sitting with Charles may begin to wonder about the clues, the signals, and the information that would help discern the level of truth to Charles's stated intent to kill his counterpart. Is this one incident merely a tip of an iceberg indicating a history and projected future of violent reactions? Is there reason to suspect abuse or violent activity at home? Perhaps this is merely adolescent bravado, all performed for the benefit of the counselor or some imaginary audience. The effective school counselor certainly listens to a student's story—but does so with a discerning ear in search of meaning.

Listening to student disclosure and attempting to make meaning of those disclosures requires a school counselor to employ a model, a guide, and an orienting framework that places this disclosure into some meaningful context. The current text focuses upon the use of a cognitive-orienting framework to guide this discernment, this search for meaning.

In the chapters that follow, the reader will be introduced to the specific theoretical constructs, intervention strategies, and research supporting the efficacy of a cognitive approach to school counseling. However, prior to getting into the theory and application of a cognitive model of school counseling, it is important to first highlight the value of a reflective process and meaning making for all counselors, regardless of theoretical orientation.

COUNSELOR REFLECTIONS
GUIDING PRACTICE DECISIONS

The counselor's ability to reflect on his or her counseling has been identified as an essential component to effective practice (Nelson & Neufeldt, 1998). This reflection provides the counselor the means to make sense of all the data presented by a student and to connect those data with a specific counselor response both at the macrolevel of treatment planning and at the microlevel of moment-to-moment interaction that occurs within a session.

Reflection at the Macrolevel:
Case Conceptualization and Treatment Planning

It is clear that not all student information is of equal value or importance to the process and outcome of the counseling. The effective school counselor reflects on the student's disclosures and formulates these data into a coherent, yet tentative, conceptualization of what is, what is desired, and how to move from "A" to "B."

For example, consider the situation of the student who is unmotivated and as a result failing academically. Perhaps the school counselor has worked with numerous students who present as "nonmotivated," and as a result, have failing grades. While the problem is labeled with the same term, "nonmotivated," the cause for this lack of motivation is idiosyncratic to that student and thus the intervention employed must similarly be shaped in response to the uniqueness of that individual. The effective school counselor reflects upon the data at his or her disposal to shape the best intervention possible for any one student, at any one time. This process of reflection effectively links the student's presenting problem to an intervention plan.

This planning and reflective practice is not a static, one-time process; rather, it refers to the thinking that takes place following a session or an encounter that allows the counselor to review what he or she did, what he or she anticipated would happen, and what in fact did happen. From the initial meeting through the end of any one "contract," the effective school counselor must gather and analyze case information, formulate new hypotheses, and develop and implement intervention decisions (Tillett, 1996).

Reflection at the Microlevel: Reflection "in" Process

While it is essential to use student data to develop case conceptualization and intervention plans, school counselors know that counseling is a dynamic process and cannot be staged in nice linear steps. School counselors appreciate that while they may be prepared with a well-thought plan and a well-stocked "intervention toolbox," these cannot simply be applied in a one-size-fits-all approach. The subtleties of each relationship, the unique characteristics of both participants, and the context of time and place all contribute to the need for counselors to fine-tune and adjust these plans, and often devise strategies right at the moment of interaction.

Counseling as a reflective process is one in which the counselor is simultaneously involved in the design and implementation of action, "[. . .] while at the same time remaining detached enough to observe and feel the action that is occurring, and to respond" (Tremmel, 1993, p. 436). Consider the simple example of offering a tissue to a tearful student. What is the intent of such a gesture? While such a gesture appears perhaps caring and helpful, might it signal that tears are not allowed? Could offering the tissue highlight and thus sensitize a student who feels somewhat embarrassed by the tears? Is this the purpose of the activity?

The reflective counselor knows what he or she expected to achieve by this gesture and will rapidly process the student's reactions, contrasting it to what was expected, and adjust accordingly. Therefore, the counselor who is providing the tissue as invitation to share feelings may note the student's dismissal of that invitation and, in turn, simply state, "Ginny, you seem upset. Would you like to tell me what's going on?" Or, perhaps the counselor offers the tissues as a simple physical comfort, but notes that the client becomes embarrassed by the counselor's recognition of the apparent upset. Under these conditions, the counselor may simply lower the box and place it on the table, redirecting the student with the comment, "Ginny, I'm glad you are here. Have a seat (pointing to a chair) and make yourself comfortable." These are not actions that can be prescribed nor even anticipated, but require the rapid processing of data and comparison of *what is* to *what was hoped for*, with the end result being an adjustment of counselor action.

When "What Is" Fails to Match the "What Was Expected"

Essential to reflective practice is the counselor's awareness of a disparity between what is and what is expected. Understanding that the student's current situation is not the preferred scenario stimulates the counselor to reflect on the data at hand in order to generate intervention plans to facilitate the student's movement toward the desired outcome. This happens both at the macrolevel as the counselor develops a case conceptualization and treatment plan, and at the microlevel as the counselor adjusts his or her own actions in response to the student's reactions at any one moment within a session. But how does a counselor know what to expect? What are the standards—the measures—against which to contrast actual events to expected events and outcomes?

While there is no single set of universal markers of what should be expected at any one point in our counseling, expectations of what "should be" can be established as outgrowth of the counselor's model or orienting framework. Our counseling models not only place the student's issues within a meaningful context, but also establish what to expect when stimuli for change are introduced (Irving & Williams, 1995).

ORIENTING FRAMEWORKS GUIDING REFLECTION

Developing plans that reflect the needs and resources of the individual student, and then adjusting the processes of our counseling in response to the subtleties and nuances of the encounter are characteristics of the reflective practitioner. And while such reflective practice may be both intuitively appealing and empirically supported, it is not an easy process to implement.

Take a moment and reflect on your first experience as a counselor-in-training. For many of us this first encounter occurred in a fundamentals course or a helping-relationship lab where we met with a volunteer "client" or classmate. Whatever the nature and setting of this initial encounter, it is quite possible that you found yourself engulfed in an overabundance of specific information, having no real sense of how to organize it or how to employ it in order to move your "client" in any direction. To expect that you, as counselor-in-training, would employ reflective practice would be unrealistic. In our early stages of training, we lacked standards or guides to contrast that which "is" with that which was "desired." We lacked an assimilated model or framework to guide our understanding and expectations of the counseling process.

So, prior to making any meaningful reflections and procedural decisions, the effective school counselor needs a framework—a schema—or a rough template to help make sense of the data being gathered. Without such an orienting framework or theory, we truly can become "directionless creatures bombarded with literally hundreds of impressions and pieces of information in a single session" (Prochaska & Norcross, 1994, p. 3).

A Process Needing Structure

Most of us can follow directions to assemble a toy or build a simple structure. Opening the package, we usually look for the directions for quick and easy assembly. The instructions sheets often identify all the parts included, the tools required, and even the steps to take (pictures help!). Even simple "problems" like putting a puzzle together, while not providing step-by-step instructions, make it easier by providing a picture of the finished product on the box top. Knowing the parts and having a concept of how they go together certainly makes assembly that much easier.

While many who work in a problem-solving capacity are presented with problems that are structured with linear steps leading to solutions, this is not true of the world of the school counselor. We in the counseling field are presented with situations that often have no clear beginning, ending, nor certainly predictable—linear—steps toward resolution.

The upset student standing in our door comes neither with easily identified parts nor clear step-by-step instructions. Using our attending and questioning skills allows us to quickly open our "student package." However, unlike most projects that have clearly marked parts, our student provides many pieces—many items and many points of contact that come flowing out into our session, all without the benefit of a parts' list or assembly instruction. Which parts are important and which are redundant or unnecessary? Where does one start? What comes next? How do we put "a" to "b"? These questions are typically answered in the instructions provided by manufactures, but are clearly absent when the "project" is helping a student navigate his or her life crisis.

Reflecting on what the student has shared and how he or she shares it—all in the context of the complexity of the human experience, and within a specific time and place of the encounter—requires some guide, some format, or some structure, or else it will be simply overwhelming. If only one had the picture on the box or the detailed instructions of where to start and how to proceed!

While there is no one picture or set of detailed instructions to guide us with our counseling, the utilization of an organizational framework will help the counselor organize the data, make conceptual connections, find themes, and provide purposeful linkages to goals and interventions.

THE COGNITIVE THEORY:
A VALUABLE ORIENTING FRAMEWORK

Cognitive theory provides a useful organizational framework for case conceptualization, intervention planning, and implementation. Case studies employing developmentally appropriate adjustment to cognitive intervention strategies have pointed to the utility of this approach, even with young students (e.g., Choate-Summers et al., 2008; Kendall et al., 2008; Stallard, 2002). While much of the current research joins behavioral and cognitive strategies into cognitive-behavioral therapy, the goal of this book is to present the cognitive model as a distinct, orienting framework. The position taken here, and that articulated by Judith Beck (1995), is that cognitive therapy is defined not by the types of techniques the therapist uses, but rather by the therapist's planning and implementing treatment *according to a cognitive formulation and conceptualization.*

Thus—as is true for all of the books in this series—the current book will present specific techniques and intervention strategies, but will place primary emphasis on illustrating the value of a cognitive-orienting framework to guide school counselors' reflective practice and their formulation of case conceptualizations and treatment plans. With this as the point of focus for the text, we turn to a presentation of the fundamental philosophy and core principles guiding cognitive practice (Chapter 2), prior to presenting specific strategies and intervention techniques for school counselors' use with a cognitive-orienting framework.

SUMMARY

Counselors in Search of Meaning

- Listening to student disclosure, and attempting to make meaning of those disclosures, requires that a school counselor employ a model, a guide, and an orienting framework to place these disclosures into some meaningful context.

Counselor Reflections Guiding Practice Decisions

- The counselor's ability to reflect on his or her counseling has been identified as an essential component of effective practice.
- Reflection provides the counselor the means to make sense of all the data presented by a student and to connect those data with a counselor response and interventions.

Orienting Frameworks Guiding Reflection

- Counselors work with ill-structured problems; they are ill-structured in that they lack linear steps leading to solutions.
- A counselor's theory, model, or orienting framework provides the "structure" needed to begin to understand the large amount of information gathered in counseling and that understanding is used to formulate effective intervention plans.

Cognitive Approach: A Valuable Orienting Framework

- The position taken here is that cognitive therapy is defined not by the types of techniques the therapist uses, but rather by the therapist's planning and implementing treatment according to a cognitive formulation and conceptualization.
- Research has pointed to the utility of a cognitive approach to counseling even with younger students.

NOTE

1. All client names and reference materials reflect composite cases and not a single actual student.

The Fundamental Principles of Cognitive Theory

2

It could be argued that the philosophic origins of a cognitive approach to counseling started with the Stoic philosophers, including Epictetus and Marcus Aurelius. Epictetus wrote in *The Enchiridion*, "Men are disturbed not by things, but by the view which they take of them" (first century A.D./1955). This, in a nutshell, is the fundamental "truth" that serves as the keystone of a cognitive-orienting framework.

While theorists such as Alfred Adler, George Kelly, and Albert Ellis provide the contemporary roots for a cognitive approach, it was Aaron Beck who, in the midsixties, developed an approach to the treatment of depression that he termed "cognitive" therapy. Beck and those who have followed (see the work of David Burns (1999) and Arthur Freeman and colleagues [2004]) offer a range of subtle and nuanced adaptations of a cognitive approach to counseling. The current chapter will present the underlying philosophy, principles, assumptions, and constructs of a cognitive approach to school counseling.

FUNDAMENTAL PRINCIPLES AND OPERATIONAL ASSUMPTIONS

As noted, numerous clinicians and theorists have developed approaches to counseling that have been grouped under the umbrella of a cognitive model. However, amidst this diversity and variation, the one consistency binding each of these approaches together is the emphasis given to the role that cognitive processes play as the foundation for human feeling and action. Counselors operating from a cognitive-orienting framework not only emphasize cognitions as crucial mediators in the creation and modulation of emotions and behaviors, but also generally embrace the following basic principles and assumptions.

Humans Are Meaning Makers

One of the first basic assumptions held by counselors operating with a cognitive-orienting framework is that human beings are meaning makers. This assumption posits that as we move through our day-to-day experiences, our initial response to life's events is to interpret or give meaning to these experiences. Whether it is a young child encountering a dog for the first time, or you or I hearing a noise in the dark, the first response to these encounters is to seek an answer to the question, "What is (was) that?"

Humans Create Schemata

As experiences, for example encountering dogs, are repeated, we develop templates or patterns to help us interpret and respond rapidly, with minimal effortful thought to these experiences. These templates, or schemata (Piaget, 1985), are actively created over the course of our development and act as lenses through which our life events are processed and analyzed. These schemata are mental structures, or patterns, and reflect the way a person configures self, the world, the past, and the future. These schemata, while grounded in the present, are based on past experiences. Thus, a student who has a lengthy experience of abuse and rejection may develop cognitive schemata that result in seeing himself as "rejectable" and the world as a "dangerous, abusive place." Or, consider the case of a child who, because of early life experience and feedback from others, believes that she is not very smart and is likely to fail at specific types of tasks (e.g., mathematics, public speaking, sports, etc.). This child may develop a schema that has two very significant impacts. First, this child may approach life events with the self-percept of being inadequate and thus likely to fail. Under these conditions, this student will have an increased sensitivity to, and awareness of, data that fits this schema while filtering out or distorting contradictory data. She may have gone through the day making many successful decisions, performing well in her classes, and yet with this schema, she is likely to remember only encountering failures, while filtering out any evidence of success or discounting these successes as merely insignificant things that anyone could do.

This process of filtering experience so that only those that "fit" the schema of being "inadequate, a failure," while distorting or filtering out those that fail to match this existing schema, continues to strengthen the operational-assumptive schemata. A second outcome of such an assumptive system that results in the prediction one will fail even before attempting the task is that this belief may result in behaviors (e.g., nonachieving, failure-avoiding actions) and feelings (e.g., depression, anxiety) that may actually interfere with her success. In this case, the schema doesn't just filter reality—it serves as a base for a self-fulfilling prophecy where the prophecy is made by the person and then enacted, thus creating reality.

As may be obvious, the goal for a counselor working with a student in this situation would be to assist the student in identifying (see Chapter 4) and then modifying (see Chapter 5) his or her dysfunctional schemata or assumptive systems, and then transforming the student's meaning making for increased adaptability and functionality.

Cognitions Are Mediators

Central to a cognitive orientation is the assumption that thoughts, beliefs, attitudes, and perceptual biases influence what emotions will be experienced as well as the intensity of those emotions. That is, an individual's affect and behavior is largely determined by the way in which he or she structures, or gives meaning, to his or her experiences.

The process is as simple as A-B-C (Prochaska & Norcross, 1994) (see Figure 2.1).

Figure 2.1   The A-B-C Connection

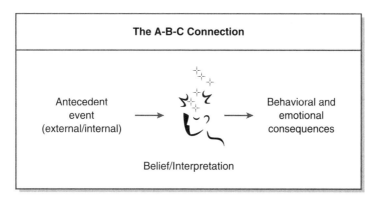

That is, at point A, there are "activating events of life," and these represent the antecedent event, such as receiving a notice of employment termination or the announcement of low SAT score. At Point B this event is "interpreted" or given meaning. Point B represents the beliefs that individuals use in order to process and make meaning out of these antecedent events and all events of their lives. Point C reflects the affective and behavioral consequences of embracing the beliefs at B.

While this basic "principle," or assumption, may be as simple as A-B-C, embracing the realities that our emotions are most often the result of our own interpretative cognitions, and not the direct response to life events, is not something that happens easily. The school counselor working from a cognitive-orienting framework appreciates this and promotes the understanding and acceptance of this thought-feeling connection (see Chapter 3) as one of the early goals in counseling. As will be discussed in Chapter 3, helping a student gain this understanding, this insight, into the "causative role" of his or her thinking to feelings and behavior is not an easy process, especially in light of the many messages he, she, and we have received, which encourage us to believe that feelings are the result of outside events rather than our interpretations of these events. This point and strategies useful for facilitating acceptance of this principle will be discussed in detail in Chapter 3.

Cognitions Can Be Functional and Dysfunctional

To successfully function and adapt to the demands of one's life, a person's schemata must correspond to conditions as they actually are, and/or clearly provide the sense of reality that is functional and adaptive for that person. The beliefs, cognitions, and schemata one employs to give meaning to life experiences can be rational and functional, and thus result in emotional and behavioral consequences (at point C) that seem to help him or her respond to the activating events in useful ways. For example, the student receiving notice of the poor SAT scores, while perhaps sad and a bit nervous about the impact of these scores on her college acceptances, may find that these emotions serve as good motivation for: (1) taking the SAT preparation course, and (2) writing a letter to the college admissions office asking for a personal interview. Both of these actions—these behaviors— seem to be potentially useful in that they may increase her chances of being accepted. However, the beliefs, at point B, can also be irrational and dysfunctional. This would be the case when they are *not* accurate reflections of the event or its potential impact and *do not* result in helpful feelings and behaviors at point C (consequences). Consider the student who, in receiving notification of poor SAT scores, concludes: (1) I'll never get into college; (2) Everyone will avoid me for being so dumb, or (3) I will never amount to anything of value. With this interpretation of the data received, the student may begin to feel hopeless and helpless and truly expect her life to be miserable from that point forward. With these as her core beliefs and feelings, behaviors such as drug and alcohol use or even suicide may seem to be the only solution to escape this horrible life. Clearly, these behaviors are not only nonuseful and nonfunctional ways for improving SAT scores or increasing the chance of getting into college, but more tragically, they unnecessarily place the student in more pain than the original disappointment regarding the poor scores.

As illustrated by our SAT example, individuals can use good and straight logic alongside data processing to interpret day-to-day events, or alternatively, can distort the meaning and real impact of these events, and with such distortion create feelings and behaviors that are not the most effective and functional in that particular situation. Whether it is by the nature of our design or the creation of our cultures, our cognitions can be functional, serving the purpose desired by the individual (and society), or dysfunctional, blocking or at least failing to support one's function and adaptation. In trying to discern the functionality and/or rationality of a client's thinking, Maultsby (1984) proposed the following criteria:

1. Rational thinking is based on obvious facts.

2. Rational thinking best helps people protect their lives and health.

3. Rational thinking best helps people achieve their own short-term and long-term goals.

4. Rational thinking best helps people avoid their most unwanted conflicts with other people.

5. Rational thinking best helps people feel emotionally the way they want to feel without using alcohol or other drugs.

Schemata Are Resistant to Change

Changing or modifying a student's maladaptive schemata seems like a reasonable goal, but it is not a goal that is easily nor readily accomplished. A student's schemata have and continue to serve as the mechanisms through which he or she makes sense of experience. Once established, a student's schemata are difficult to change, even when change is desired by the student. This is an important point to remember. Schemata shape our sense of reality and changing that personal reality is a difficult task. This appears to be a simple artifact of the way schemas are formed and maintained.

Jean Piaget (1985) postulated the process by which humans take new experiences and make meaning by either incorporating the new experience into an existing schema in a process called "assimilation," or by creating an entirely new structure, a new schema, or dramatically adjusting an existing one in a process he termed "accommodation." This second process of accommodation—modifying old schemata or creating new ones—requires more psychic energy and, as such, it is not the first choice as we try to adapt to new circumstances. In fact, we tend to resist accommodating to new experiences, choosing rather to reshape our experiences so that they can be processed through existing schemata. As such, we may embrace information that confirms our assumptions and schemata and either ignore or distort those data that are nonconfirmatory. Consider the infant who learns to associate certain features with the construct "bow-wow" (or dog). That child, when first encountering another furry, small animal, may process the new experience through the schema of dog and refer to the animal as a "bow-wow." However, perhaps future experience will highlight features of this new animal that do not neatly fit into the dog schema and cannot be simply overlooked or ignored. Under these conditions, the child will experience cognitive tension and it is this tension, this cognitive dissonance, that will motivate the creation of a new schema for interpreting this experience.

The same is true for a depressed student who sees himself as hopeless, helpless, and worthless. If a friend attempts to point out data that is non-confirming to the student's self-percepts, such as, "Look Tom, you have some good friends and you get good grades and you made the baseball team," the student who is locked into this hopeless, helpless, and worthless schema may attempt to distort the message rather than accept this information as evidence that his belief of being worthless is not valid. He may respond, "Are you kidding? Look, I haven't gotten honors since freshman year; I can't find a date for the prom, and in baseball, I'm sitting on the bench hardly ever playing!"

It is important to understand that the student in this case doesn't want to be depressed nor does he want to retain his depressive schemata. However, the student's depressive schemata and the resulting view of self and his life are his "realities," and it is our tendency to defend our view of reality against nonconfirming experiences, even when this view, these schemata, result in personal pain.

It is clear that achieving significant change in one's assumptive view of the world will almost always meet with some resistance, and when achieved, occurs with concomitant emotional reactions. It is also clear that emotional distress, in and of itself, is insufficient for modifying these assumptions. It appears that we are more motivated to adjust "reality" in order to have it fit our schemata, our assumptive filters, rather than adjust those assumptions to more adequately reflect our reality.

The school counselor operating with a cognitive-orienting model is aware of this protective tendency. The school counselor will employ a variety of techniques and strategies to help students challenge this tendency to protect nonadaptive schemata and reformulate these schemata so that they result in more functional feelings and actions.

Cognitions Can Be Modified

While there is theory and research (Dattilio, 2006; Ellis, 2002) that suggests that individuals work hard *not* to change schemata and cognitions, choosing rather to modify experience so that it fits (assimilates) existing schemata, the truth is that cognitions *can* be modified. In situations where the student is unable to simply adjust the world to fit the assumption, he or she will be motivated by the cognitive dissonance (i.e., tension) experienced to reexamine his or her basic assumptions, and embrace more reliable and functional guides.

The school counselor operating from a cognitive-orienting framework believes:

1. Through counseling, students can become aware of their dysfunctional thoughts and cognitive distortions.

2. Students can be taught to shift from self-defeating, dysfunctional thoughts and attitudes to self-enhancing, functional thoughts.

3. Correction of these faulty dysfunctional constructs can lead to more adaptive and functional ways to respond to the lived experience.

Cognitive Change Requires Work

When looking at the A-B-Cs of a cognitive approach (see Figure 2.1), one may conclude that identifying a student's schemata and adjusting these schemata is an easy process. It is not unusual to find students, and some counselors, who believe that counselors operating with a cognitive-orienting framework simply help students say nice, positive things to themselves as a way of attacking depression, anxiety, sadness, loneliness, and other debilitating experiences. Wrong!

Just "thinking positively" is not going to permanently affect change in self-percepts and worldviews, and thus, any benefits will be short-lived. For example, a depressed student may be encouraged to say self-affirming statements, but for the depression to be attacked, the negative thoughts, beliefs, and assumptions that perpetuate the depressed mood need to be identified, challenged, and reformed. Cognitive change requires work and the counselor with a cognitive orientation is continuously active, and deliberately interactive, with the student to challenge and reformulate beliefs and perceptions.

The school counselor employing a cognitive-orienting framework takes an active role in the process of counseling. The focus of the counseling is "here-and-now," with the major thrust given toward investigating the student's thinking and feeling "in" practice as well as between sessions.

The student must be helped to: (1) identify his or her dysfunctional thoughts, processing bias and beliefs; (2) learn to actively debate these as simply unsupported; and then (3) embrace the reformulation that results from this challenge to the original schema with new nonconfirmatory data. This process may require that the student learn new skills and strategies to help monitor his or her stream of thought, identify beliefs and attitudes, and subject these to the laws of reason.

Counseling from a cognitive orientation involves learning a new internal language—a new way of processing information. It is a new fundamental philosophy of life. And, as is true for all complex learning, this takes work!

COGNITIVE THERAPY FOR SCHOOL-AGED CHILDREN

Since a primary ingredient of cognitive counseling involves psycho-education into the actual model being employed, it is essential that students have sufficient cognitive and emotional development to: (1) reflect on and describe their own feelings and thoughts, (2) discriminate amongst their thoughts, their feelings, and their behaviors, and (3) examine cause-effect relations between these (Reynolds, Girling, Coker, & Eastwood, 2006). Given the "cognitive tasks" involved in counseling from a cognitive orientation, one may question whether it is useful and effective for school-aged children.

A primary concern sometimes raised is whether young children, those under age 10, can actually understand and engage in the somewhat "abstract" concepts employed in a cognitive approach. In response to these concerns, there is evidence that young children are indeed capable of such cognitive reflections. Research has demonstrated that children can discriminate between thoughts and feelings (Quakley, Coker, Palmer, & Reynolds, 2003); discriminate amongst thoughts, feelings, and behaviors (Quakley, Reynolds, & Coker, 2004); and also link thoughts and feelings, and make post-event attributions (Doherr, Reynolds, Wetherly, & Evans, 2005). Further, case studies employing developmentally appropriate adjustment to intervention strategies have pointed to the utility of this approach with young children (e.g., Stallard, 2002).

School counselors operating with a cognitive-orienting framework employ numerous techniques—including expressive techniques, games, and workbooks—as a way to address the uniqueness of their students' levels of cognitive development and to increase the possibility of engaging the student in this approach to helping. As will be demonstrated throughout the upcoming chapters, these materials and techniques remain theoretically faithful and thus can be integrated under the theoretical umbrella of a cognitive approach to counseling.

SUMMARY

The A-B-C Connection

- Central to a cognitive orientation is the assumption that thoughts, beliefs, attitudes, and perceptual biases influence what emotions will be experienced as well as the intensity of those emotions.

Humans as Meaning Makers

- As we move through our day-to-day experiences, our initial response to life's events is to interpret or give meaning to the experience.
- We create templates or schemata to help us interpret and respond rapidly, with minimal effortful thought to these experiences.

Cognitions as Mediators

- An individual's affect and behavior is largely determined by the way in which he or she structures, or gives meaning, to his or her experiences.

Cognitions Are Functional and Dysfunctional

- The beliefs, cognitions, and schemata one employs to give meaning to life experiences can be rational and functional, and thus result in emotional and behavioral consequences that seem to help the individual respond to the activating events in useful ways.
- Beliefs, cognitions, and schemata can also be irrational and dysfunctional when they are not accurate reflections of the event or its potential impact, and these do not result in helpful, adaptive feelings and behaviors.

Schemata Are Resistant to Change

- Schemata, once established, are difficult to change.
- In adapting to new experiences, we first attempt to "assimilate" the new experience into our existing schemata, and only when that is not possible will we develop new schemata through the process of accommodation.

(Continued)

(Continued)

- We tend to resist accommodating to new experiences, embracing information that confirms our assumptions and schemata and either ignore or distort those data that are nonconfirmatory.

Cognitions Are Adjustable

- In situations where students are unable to simply adjust the world to fit the assumption, they will be motivated by the cognitive dissonance (tension) they experience to reexamine their basic assumptions and embrace more reliable and functional guides.

Cognitive Change Requires Work

- Cognitive change requires work and the counselor with a cognitive orientation is continuously active and deliberately interactive with the student in a process to challenge and reformulate beliefs and perceptions.
- The school counselor helps students identify their dysfunctional thoughts, processing bias and beliefs; learn to actively debate these as simply unsupported, and then embrace the reformulation that results from this challenge to the original schemata with new nonconfirmatory data.

Cognitive Counseling for School-Aged Children

- There is evidence that young children can discriminate between thoughts and feelings; discriminate amongst thoughts, feelings and behaviors; link thoughts and feelings, and make post-event attributions.

Part II

Targets and Techniques of Cognitive Counseling

A s is true of all school counselors, regardless of model or orientation, the school counselor utilizing a cognitive framework values the creation and maintenance of a working alliance with his or her student. The school counselor working from a cognitive-orienting framework employs those fundamental communication and relationship-building skills noted as core to a therapeutic relationship.

However, once the "work" of counseling begins, the school counselor with a cognitive orientation turns his or her attention to the identification and correction of the faulty thinking contributing to the problem at hand. To this end, the school counselor will employ a wide array of techniques. The school counselor with a cognitive orientation may engage directive or reflective modes, implement scientific-didactic principles or empathic, nondirective methods, and call upon a variety of educational materials including readings, workbooks, and videos—all geared to assist the student in identifying and correcting faulty thinking.

While the upcoming chapters will provide a look at specific strategies employed by school counselors utilizing a cognitive orientation, emphasis is given to the unique way a cognitive orientation guides the counselor's thinking and decision making in regards to work with a particular student. As the school counselor moves from initial contact through termination of the formal helping relationship, he or she will use a number of goals, or targets, that will serve as markers to guide practice.

The first "target," or goal, for a cognitively oriented counselor is the development of the student's understanding and "ownership" of the connection between thoughts and feelings (Chapter 3). With this awareness and value on the pivotal role of thoughts, beliefs, and schemata in the formation of both functional and dysfunctional responses, the counselor turns his or her attention to assisting the student in identifying those personal cognitions and beliefs that appear to be at the root of the student's current difficulties (Chapter 4). The final target (Chapter 5) for the school counselor employing a cognitive orientation is to engage the student in the reformulation of the cognitions and underlying beliefs so that the student's cognitions result in more functional, adaptive processing of life experiences.

Each of these "targets" can serve as markers to guide progression through the counseling process. The "what" and "how" of reaching these milestones are detailed in the chapters found within Part II. However, prior to proceeding, one caveat is in order. As with all techniques described in counseling books, the interventions presented gain value by way of their masterful timing and application at the hands of the effective school counselor. Just as a child may be able to make a sound with a simple slide whistle, in the hands of a musician this simple instrument can produce beautiful music. The same is true for the discourse and strategies employed in cognitive-oriented school counseling. With practice, supervisory feedback, and engagement in reflection, these techniques move from being simply paper narratives to become valuable tools within your own repertoire of counseling strategies.

Helping the Student 3
to Understand
and Embrace the
Thought-Feeling
Connection

"I get what you are saying about my thinking but you have to understand how much he really pisses me off!"

—Edward, age 15

The words spoken by Edward, a tenth-grade student, to his counselor not only give evidence of this student's anger, but also reveal the difficulty most of us have in truly embracing the connection of thoughts and feelings. The principles and operating assumptions identified in Chapter 2 are clear and straightforward. Hopefully, as you read through the chapter, you were able to say, "Oh, yes, I get it." However, to be effective, these principles need to be embraced and not just conceptually "gotten."

Moving a student from the point where he or she conceptually *gets* the concept of thoughts as mediator to feelings and behaviors to a point where he or she actually *owns* the principle as a personal reality is neither automatic nor easy. Achieving this first goal in the process of cognitively oriented counseling requires the school counselor's artistic hand to employ reflections, questions, summarization, confrontations, and directed activities in an attempt to facilitate the student's understanding and ownership of the thought-feeling connection. It is this process and the strategies employed that serve as the focus of this chapter.

COGNITIONS AS MEDIATORS
OF FEELINGS AND ACTIONS

The school counselor employing a cognitive-orienting framework maintains that the way an individual evaluates situations or events is the primary determiner of affect and behavior. The importance or value of this perspective is not merely academic. This position provides the counselor and student with a sense of hope and real empowerment. If we, and our students, approach our issues of concern, believing that our feelings and behaviors are intricately and directly tied to life's events, we may find ourselves in the position of victim—trapped in our feelings and behaviors until the events change. However, if we accept the position that our feelings and actions are the result of the meaning we give to these life events, then changing these feelings and behaviors is as "simple" as changing our view of the events and circumstances we encounter.

This is not to suggest we should delude ourselves into thinking things are great when they are not, or that there is no problem when there is. The point, which will be further explicated, is that when our feelings and actions appear to inhibit us from making the best of situations or from employing the most effective strategies for problem solving and adapting to these events, then, under these conditions, we may want to reconsider our viewpoint on the issue at hand. Consider the cases of Tom and Brad as each responds to the experience of having his girlfriend end their relationship.

Tom and Brad are both seniors in high school. Each has come to the counselor's office expressing upset about the fact that he had just been "dumped" by his girlfriend. However, there is a significant difference in the intensity of each boy's emotional response and the "adaptive" quality of their actions.

Tom is devastated. His grades are falling dramatically; he is having difficulty getting out of bed and has been missing school. Tom explained that he doesn't want to go out or hang out with his friends, and that he finds very little enjoyment in those activities, such as going to the mall, playing video games, etc., which he previously enjoyed. In reviewing Tom's situation, the counselor finds that the initial problem of being "dumped" by his girlfriend has taken on broader and more intense implications. This expansion of the problem becomes more understandable as we listen to Tom's assessment of this situation. From Tom's point of view, his depression is not just the result of losing his girlfriend, Linda, but the belief that the ending of this one specific relationship is evidence (for Tom) that he will be alone for the rest of his life, and that he is a "loser." Tom's "logic" is that if this one person couldn't love him . . . no one ever could! His perception of his future is one of total loneliness, certainly a devastating projection.

Contrast this to Brad's viewpoint and interpretation of the "meaning" of the ending of his relationship. Brad is truly upset; he is sad and is finding it difficult to stay focused on his schoolwork. He forces himself to come to school, and even though he lacks a desire for hanging out with his friends, he pushes himself to do so. Brad is able to express his sadness, and even some confusion and concern about what he could have done differently to maybe save the relationship. Brad has engaged with his friends seeking both advice and comfort. When discussing his relationship, he states that he believed that they had a good relationship, although as he talks about it, he is able to recognize that it wasn't perfect. According to Brad, they did seem to be disagreeing a lot about things to do, and Brad was feeling a bit "trapped" and unable to maintain his relationships with his guy friends.

In these situations, one could argue that while the event—getting "dumped"—was similar for both Brad and Tom, the impact was significantly more severe for Tom. If the events were relatively similar, how does one account for the differential responses observed? It is clear that the differential impact was the result of the way each student processed the meaning and long-term effect of the event.

AN IDEA DIFFICULT TO EMBRACE

While it is relatively easy to provide case illustrations to highlight the role of thoughts, as mediator, between events and emotional and behavioral consequences, it is not that easy to "convince" the student that the source of his pain, his upset, is truly himself and not the external conditions in which he finds himself. The belief that "it is me that upsets me," rather than, "you or it is upsetting me," is truly a foreign concept for the twenty-first century student. Consider the case of Ricardo.

Ricardo, a sixth-grade student known for his drive and high achievement, has been referred to the counselor's office because of his recent outburst in class. Apparently, Ricardo lost control and began to yell obscenities and throw his books on the ground in response to his teacher failing to choose him to come to the board and answer the "challenge" problem. When asked by his counselor to describe what happened, Ricardo explained that he had his hand raised and that he really was the first one with his hand up. He then complained that Mrs. Johnson (his teacher), "never calls on me!"

Ricardo truly believes that his outburst was justified and understandable in light of what he believed was Mrs. Johnson's total disregard for him as a student, and as a person. From Ricardo's perspective, it was all her fault; *she made him mad.* Ricardo believes that his anger is not only a direct response to his teacher's failure to recognize his efforts, but is justified given her unfairness.

The school counselor working with Ricardo will, most likely, find any attempts to redefine the source of the anger as resting within Ricardo's own thinking falling on deaf ears and a resistant mind. Ricardo firmly believes that the activating event of the teacher ignoring him and calling on another student directly resulted in the emotional and behavioral consequences observed. However, perhaps the school counselor could open Ricardo's thinking by presenting an alternative scenario, one where the teacher's action remains the same, but where Ricardo provides a different interpretation or meaning to the teacher's action, and as such, results in a different emotional and behavioral response.

Counselor: Ricardo, let me ask you to think about a situation that is a little different. Let's pretend that you are in class, just like today, and you are raising your hand, but right before your teacher picks a student to come to the board, you remember that your pants are ripped in the back, you know, the seat of your pants. Okay (smiling)?

Ricardo: Yeah (smiling).

Counselor: Let's pretend that the teacher calls on William, who is sitting right next to you, and she says, "William, would you please come up to the board and show us how to solve the challenge problem?" How do you think you would feel?

Ricardo: Okay, I guess.

Counselor: And how would you act? Behave?

Ricardo: I would just put my hand down, and sit back and watch William.

Counselor: Great. But I'm a little confused. I mean, after all, here it is the same situation that is your teacher selecting another student to come to the board, and yet the consequences are really different? I mean, you are calm and attentive. What's changed?

Ricardo: I don't know.

Counselor: Well, why do you think you would be okay not going to the board?

Ricardo: 'Cause I have a hole in my pants, and if I was at the board everyone would see my butt, and that would be embarrassing.

Counselor: Oh, so you are calm because rather than sitting there and saying to yourself things like, "She never calls on me," or, "This isn't fair," you were thinking, "Whew! I'm glad she didn't call on me. That hole in my pants is embarrassing." Does that sound right?

Ricardo: Yeah, I guess, but she really got me mad. I mean, it's not fair!

As illustrated by these examples of Ricardo, Brad, and Tom, the source of each of their feelings rests in meaning assigned and severity of consequences assumed by each of the students. This is truly the power of cognitions as mediator. However, it is a truth, as illustrated by Ricardo's last response, which we do not readily embrace.

There are numerous examples within our own day-to-day experiences that illustrate the many ways our culture promotes the idea that our emotional experiences are the direct result of life's events. It is almost a cultural pastime to blame others for our upset. People, young and old, are quick to point to another's comment, or the failure to get a certain grade or promotion, or even the unexpected traffic jam, as the source of their upset. With such prevalence and pervasiveness of this culturally supported idea that our unhappiness is caused by outside sources, convincing a student to own the thought-feeling connection is, at least initially, an uphill battle. The school counselor operating with a cognitive orientation appreciates this challenge while at the same time understanding that this "reeducation" of the student is essential if the counseling is to be effective.

PROMOTING UNDERSTANDING OF THE ROLE AND IMPORTANCE OF COGNITION

Helping a student understand the centrality of thinking to feeling is truly a challenge for the school counselor operating with a cognitive orientation. There are no simple, singular approaches to accomplish this task. The counselor is invited to employ all of his or her creativity and resources to engage the student in the development of this insight.

Most students will find the concept that it is one's thoughts that cause feelings contradictory to what they have grown to believe and hold to be true. Appreciating that fact, the school counselor with a cognitive orientation will go slow and employ multiple strategies to make this point clear and undeniable. Throughout the early stages of counseling, the school counselor will attempt various interventions, all geared to not only illustrate the thought-feeling connection but make it personal to the student so that the student truly encounters an "ah, ha" experience. For the counseling to be effective, the student needs to not only understand the connection of thoughts and feelings but also see the personal relevance and application within his or her own life. What follows are a number of the more common strategies used to achieve this first goal of cognitively oriented school counseling.

A Simple "Test" to View Events From Multiple Perspectives

One strategy that may prove useful in highlighting the thinking-feeling connection is to invite the student to respond to the items presented in Table 3.1. The counselor, would provide the student with the list and ask the student to look at the events listed and then identify the feelings believed to have led to each of the interpretations applied to the situation.

As the counselor and student review each situation, together they will highlight the shift in feelings that result from the shift in interpretation of the same event. The goal is to demonstrate the thought-feeling connection and the reality that the student's thoughts can create both positive and negative feelings.

Table 3.1   Thought-Feeling Connection

Event	Thought (I think . . . , therefore)	Feeling (I feel)
I got my test back and it was a 40 percent.	I'm screwed. I'm failing and my parents will kill me.	
	Ouch. I wonder if I can take a retest or do extra credit.	
My parents said that they won't pay for my car insurance.	This stinks—they promised. This is so unfair; I can't stand it!	
	I don't think I'm ready to drive.	
I didn't get an invitation to a classmate's birthday party.	Everybody's going but me. No one likes me.	
	Whew. I didn't want to go and would hate to have had to tell her.	
I was told I couldn't sit with some classmates at their lunch table.	This is horrible. I'm such a loser.	
	What's up with them? Thank goodness I can sit with. . . .	

Choosing the Feeling by Choosing the Thought

Another strategy that can be used to facilitate students' understanding of the thought-feeling connection is to have them look at a series of relevant events or experiences and then have them create an interpretation resulting in the specific feelings identified (see Table 3.2).

Table 3.2   Changing the Thought and Changing the Feeling

directions				
Directions: Read the descriptions of each of the following events and then generate "interpretations" of the event that would most likely result in each of the listed emotions.				
Event	**Irritated**	**Sad**	**Anxious**	**Curious**
I'm sitting at lunch and the girls at the other table are pointing at me and laughing!	Jerks—they think they are so special. They have no right to make fun of me.	No one likes me.	I wonder what they are saying. I wonder if they are planning to do something or embarrass me.	What's up? Did I say something or do something funny? Or are they just goofing around?
I'm standing in the recess yard and I am the last one to be picked for a team.				
The teacher told me that she wants to talk to me after school.				
I just received a college letter of rejection.				

The intent of this exercise is not to suggest that there is one right way to interpret the situation or a specific way to feel about these events, rather the hope is that the exercise will help the student come to "see" that the same "objective" event can be responded to emotionally in a variety of ways—all as a result of the meaning we place on the event.

With each of these or other such exercises, the counselor would need to engage the student in a discussion that not only continues to educate the student, but "tests" his or her understanding of this principle. Consider the dialogue between the counselor and Courtney, a third-grade student (Case Illustration 3.1). In this situation, the counselor guides the student to experience the impact of viewing a situation from an alternative perspective.

Case Illustration 3.1   Courtney: The Missing Parents

Counselor:	So, Courtney, let's imagine that it is Saturday morning and you wake up and go downstairs expecting that your mom and dad will be there. But when you get to the kitchen, you notice that they are not there. How do you think you would feel?
Courtney:	Scared.
Counselor:	Scared?
Courtney:	Yeah, they are always there. We always eat breakfast together on Saturdays. My dad makes pancakes.
Counselor:	So, you would expect them to be there since that is what usually happens. Okay, so I kind of understand why you might be surprised that they aren't there . . . but why scared?
Courtney:	I don't know, something must have happened.
Counselor:	Hmm . . . something? Like what?
Courtney:	I don't know. Maybe my mom got sick and my dad had to take her to the hospital, or maybe they went to the store and got in an accident.
Counselor:	Wow! I guess, if it was true that your mom or dad were in the hospital, that would be something to be concerned about. But are they?
Courtney:	I don't know.
Counselor:	That's right. We don't know where they are, but if we think something bad has happened, then we start to feel that way. You know, we start to get upset, scared. What type of thought could you have that would make you feel happy that they aren't in the kitchen?
Courtney:	I don't know.
Counselor:	Well, was there ever a time when your parents were busy doing something and weren't where you thought they would be?
Courtney:	You mean, like if they are working in the garden?
Counselor:	Great. So, let's imagine you come down and when you don't see your mom and dad in the kitchen, you say to yourself, "I bet they are out working in the garden." How would you feel with that thought?
Courtney:	Hungry.
Counselor:	That's funny. I bet you would be. Would you be scared or worried?
Courtney:	No . . . just surprised.
Counselor:	Isn't that wild? Here it is the same situation. You know your mom and dad are not in the kitchen when you wake up, and are not making the pancakes, but if you think, "Oh, no, they are in the hospital" then you get

	really scared, but if you think, "I bet they are in the garden," then you are just surprised and hungry!
Courtney:	Yeah, and if they are out buying donuts, I would feel really happy!
Counselor:	Courtney, that's great. You really got it! A lot of students don't understand this, but how we feel, you know worried or happy, even sad or mad, is because of how we think when we experience different things, like if we experience our mom and dad not being in the kitchen when we awake.

In this relatively simple illustration, the counselor was able to have the student identify how her catastrophic thinking, "They're in the hospital" would result in her experience of anxiety. With this as a springboard, the counselor can turn attention to helping the student to learn to review, debate, and reformulate her thoughts so that they more accurately reflect the reality of the moment, and position her to feel and respond more appropriately.

Using a Three-Column Approach (In Search of Monsters)

Another strategy that may prove helpful in facilitating the student's "insight" in regards to the thought-feeling connection is to walk the student through the application of a "three-column" approach (see Figure 3.1).

Figure 3.1   Three-Column-Approach Thought Log

Event (Describe what happened.)	Feelings (Describe how you are feeling.)	Thoughts (List all of your thoughts about the event. What does it mean? What do you expect?)
I got a 50 on a test.	Depressed and Anxious	I failed the test. (So what?) I'm going to fail the course. (And if I do?) They'll kick me out of this program. (And?) My life is ruined.
Tina said she doesn't want to go out anymore and that she's been seeing Charlie.	Angry	I can't believe this. (What does this mean?) She can't do this . . . how dare she break up with me. (So, what if she dares to?) I can't stand this. She's awful, and I hate her.

While the counselor can use this strategy to simply illustrate the thinking-feeling connection, the real value comes for the student during the process, with the true "ah, ha" experience that gives evidence that this principle has been embraced and assimilated. Consider the following case (Case Illustration 3.2) and the visual and verbal techniques this counselor employs to facilitate this insightful "ah, ha" and acceptance of the thinking-feeling connection.

Case Illustration 3.2	Audrey: Monsters in the Room or in the Head

Counselor:	Audrey, I'm very sorry that you are feeling so anxious, but I believe there is something we can do that will help.
Audrey:	Yeah, just get me out of that class so I don't have to stand up there and give that stupid presentation.
Counselor:	Well, I guess I understand how avoiding the presentation may help you feel more relaxed, but if I understood what you have been saying, it's not just this one presentation, or this one class, where you find yourself getting upset and anxious.
Audrey:	Yeah, I get kind of worked up, especially in school when we have all these tests and projects due and the prom is coming up. It just seems that there is too much going on.
Counselor:	You know, it sounds like when you think about things like the class presentation, or the prom coming up, that you get nervous?
Audrey:	Yeah . . . of course they do. I mean, they are big deals.
Counselor:	I have an idea. Let me show you something. Now, this may seem a bit silly, but it's really cool and I think it can help.
Audrey:	Okay.
Counselor:	Audrey, I know you babysit your little four-year-old brother Jason. So, let's use Jason as an example of something (taking a sheet of paper and beginning to draw). See these three columns? I'm going to label the first column as "A" for activating event. Now imagine that you are babysitting and you put Jason to bed. Okay, so let's write this down. The activating event is:

"A" Activating Event		
Four-year-old Jason is in bed.		
It's nighttime and therefore dark.		
It is also a rainy, noisy night.		

Audrey:	Yeah, like last night. I was babysitting and it was windy and rainy.
Counselor:	That's great. Now, let's imagine that after you placed him in bed and said good night you went downstairs, and within ten minutes, all of a sudden you hear him screaming and when you go up to his room you see he is crying and really, really scared!
Audrey:	I don't have to imagine. That actually happened.
Counselor:	Wow. This is something. Okay, so let's look at our columns and all the things we just described. I will put that in this third column labeled "C" for consequences.

"A" Activating Event		"C" Consequences
Four-year-old Jason is in bed. It's nighttime and therefore dark. It is also a rainy, noisy night.		Screaming Scared

Audrey:	Okay . . .
Counselor:	Now you see these things in the two columns, and these are real events. They are factual! It is dark and it is rainy and noisy and Jason is screaming and afraid. But I wonder why? What is causing his fear?
Audrey:	Well, I asked him, and he said he was afraid of the dark.
Counselor:	Oh, so Jason feels that this event (pointing to column A, the dark) is making him feel afraid, you know, causing his feelings?
Audrey:	Yeah, but that's normal, right? Kids are afraid of the dark!
Counselor:	Audrey, now here's the cool part. I bet if you ask your mom and dad and everyone else you know, "Are little four-year-old kids afraid of the dark?" I bet most will say, "Yes, of course!" But you know what . . . they're wrong!
Audrey:	Wrong (looking confused)?
Counselor:	I know this seems confusing, but stay with me. Do you know how you can sometimes hear your own thoughts, almost like there's a little voice in your head?
Audrey:	Okay (smiling).
Counselor:	No, it's okay—that's not crazy! We have to talk to ourselves. That's the way the brain is wired. We experience something and then we have to interpret or give it meaning and then we know how we want to react to it. So, let's see if we can get into Jason's brain as he is drifting off to sleep.

(Continued)

(Continued)

> So, he's lying there. It's dark and as he drifts off to sleep, he hears a noise; remember it's noisy... what you do think he says in his head?

Audrey: I don't know.

Counselor: Do you think he might say something like, "What's that?"

Audrey: Oh, yeah. I wasn't sure what you meant.

Counselor: Okay. But if you and I could hear what Jason was thinking, I wonder if after he said "What was that?" if he answered that question and made some interpretation of what the noise in the dark meant? So, if we were four-years-old and lying in the dark, and just falling asleep and we hear a noise, and our brain goes, "What's that?" What do you think we would say, or Jason might have said, to himself in response to the question, "What's that?" It's a...?

Audrey: A monster?

Counselor: Right on... I bet he may have. But now, look what happens (going back to the chart). See this middle column? I'm going to label that one "B" for beliefs, or self-talk, or meaning making. This is how we interpret the things that are happening. So for Jason, the actual event was that it was a dark, rainy and noisy night and most people would think that his fear was caused by the dark but now look... if the noise in A is interpreted as evidence that there is a monster in the room—that's in B—then guess what? It is *this* interpretation that causes the fear, not the event, and not the dark.

"A" Activating Event	"B" Belief Meaning Making, Self-Talk	"C" Consequences
Four-year-old Jason is in bed. It's nighttime and therefore dark. It is also a rainy, noisy night.	What's that? It's a Monster!	Screaming Scared

> And you know what? If there was a monster in the room... in this room... I bet you and I would be afraid. Sadly, there is no monster in the room, just in Jason's head. So he is the one actually causing his own upset, not the dark, just the faulty belief that there is a monster in the room.

Audrey: I think I get it.

Counselor: Well let's see.... let me test you (laughing).

> Okay. So Jason is going to bed; it's dark, noisy... how does he feel?

Audrey:	Afraid.
Counselor:	Wait (interrupting) . . . wait . . . wait . . . how about if it is dark and noisy, but it's December 24th? Now what might he be feeling?
Audrey:	Excited (smiling)?
Counselor:	Why?
Audrey:	Because he would think the noise is Santa and then he would be excited.
Counselor:	Isn't that wild? A noise in the dark—if we believe it's a monster—then we make ourselves afraid, and if we interpret the noise as Santa—we make ourselves excited. What do you think? Do you see, it's not the events or people in our life that make us nervous or mad or sad, but how we "see" or interpret these things.
Audrey:	My head hurts (laughing) . . . but it's cool.
Counselor:	Yes it is . . .

Given any presenting concern, the counselor will assist the student to identify the situations or conditions that appear to elicit the emotional experience and through attentive, reflecting dialogue identify the "beliefs," or the "interpretive perspective," that the student brings to the situation and which in fact create the emotional and behavioral response.

In Case Illustration 3.2, the counselor not only wanted Audrey to understand the process, but also wanted to set the condition that would facilitate her acceptance of this new philosophy. As depicted, it appears that the student's smile, in anticipation of what she believed would be the impact of thinking that the noise heard was created by "Santa," is evidence that she was starting to understand and embrace the principle of the "thinking-feeling" connection. But, this is just the first step. In this scenario, the illustration was about her brother Jason. The counselor now needs to help Audrey see the same process applies to her and her issue of concern.

FROM THEORY TO PERSONAL APPLICATION

Understanding the principle of thought as mediator to feelings and behaviors is one thing, owning it and seeing its application to one's lived experience is quite another. As noted previously, "owning" this principle and applying it to one's own lived experience is often resisted. As we continue with the case of Audrey (Case Illustration 3.3), we will note that while she was able to grasp the connection of thought to feeling as it applied to her brother's anxiety, she was not so open to its application in her own life. It is the job of the school counselor working from a cognitive orientation to find ways to bring this "truth" to the personal level.

Case Illustration 3.3	Audrey: But This Is Different

Audrey:	You know, I told my friends about the monster thing and they all think you're nuts.
Counselor:	You mean they really believe that the dark makes people afraid?
Audrey:	Yeah.
Counselor:	Well, you know, that is understandable. I mean, we seem to teach each other this kind of thinking. It seems like we are being told that our feelings are caused by others. I bet your friends have said things like, "You piss me off"?
Audrey:	My friends? That's one of my favorite phrases!
Counselor:	Well, if you really believe this, then you are saying other people cause your anger rather than, "It is me causing my anger by what I say to myself about what is happening to me."
Audrey:	I really think I get it, but there are things that are really serious and can freak me out.
Counselor:	Really? Like what type of things have the power to make you freak out?
Audrey	Are you kidding? How about the college board exams for one!
Counselor:	The college board exam? How does that make you freak out?
Audrey:	Well, it's like the most important thing in my life. If I screw that up, it would be horrible.
Counselor:	Horrible?
Audrey:	Well, like really a big deal.
Counselor:	Really a big deal?
Audrey:	Yes (getting a little annoyed). I want to go to college and this is important.
Counselor:	So, Audrey, if I use my A-B-C columns, it looks like you are saying that you have this event, you know, taking the college board exam, and a consequence, that you are really anxious and having trouble sleeping and eating. Now I certainly understand that the college board exam is something that you want to do well on, but I wonder if you are giving it a lot more importance than it deserves, or importance that really

works for you. Looking at your reaction and listening to your comments, it seems that you may be thinking (writing in the B column), "I'm going to fail and if I fail I won't go to college. If I don't go to college my life would be ruined."

"A" Activating Event	"B" Belief	"C" Consequence
I am taking my college board exam Saturday.	I'm going to fail. If I fail I won't go to college. If I don't go to college, my life would be ruined.	Given the life and death nature of my view of the test, I am extremely anxious. I can't sleep or eat.

Audrey: I know it's not the end of the world, my life's not over, but really it would be totally embarrassing. If I were the only one screwing up, I couldn't face my friends.

Counselor: Wow, so as you see it, this test and the score you get would determine whether or not you would ever be able to face your friends again? So, from your perspective, this is not just a test, just something used as one of a couple criteria for college admissions. It really is a test of whether you will ever have any friends?

Audrey: Seems kind of silly when you say it that way.

Counselor: But it doesn't feel silly, does it? It is hard to challenge our own beliefs, because that's how we see things. It simply seems true to us—true until we stop and really test the evidence.

Having the student gather data on his or her own experiences, and "analyze" those experiences in light of the specific interpretations provided by the student, facilitates this personal ownership. Thus, a counselor working with a student like Audrey may invite her to keep a log or journal in which she would employ the three-column framework. She would be asked to describe specific events encountered as well as the resulting feelings and behaviors, and also, most importantly, pay attention to the self-talk (interpretation and meaning making) that occurs during these times. The specific method used to gather these data can be informal, such as simply asking the student to take note and remember what he or she was thinking during experiences with the emotion and/or behavior of concern. Or, data collection can be achieved with a bit more structure (see Figure 3.2).

Figure 3.2   Taking Alternative Perspectives

Date or Day	Event or Situation	Feelings (100 being the maximum)	Self-Talk (Cognitions)	Other Possible Interpretations
Tuesday	I was going to lunch and Jerome, Natalie, and Raul were already in the lunchroom, sitting at the table. When they saw me coming, they got quiet and started giggling.	Anxious: 80%	What are they doing? Why are they making fun of me? Why don't they like me? This is horrible. I wish I could just disappear.	Maybe they were cutting up on something else and I just happened to walk in at the time. Maybe they are laughing about something I'm wearing? Maybe they are insecure and need to find fault with other people.

Of course, the form of such data collection needs to meet not only the needs of the counselor for collecting useful data, but also the comfort, resources, and interest of the student. Case Illustration 3.4 illustrates the counselor's adaptation of the data collection technique to make the process more "user" friendly.

| Case Illustration 3.4 | Donald: A Simple Journal |

Donald:	I'm not sure . . . that chart looks like a lot of work, and I'm not real good at doing things like that.
	(Reflecting "in" practice, the counselor moves toward a more informal method of data collection.)
Counselor:	I guess when you first see something like this, it does seem like it may take some time to use. How about this? Are there times in the day—perhaps in the morning before classes or later in the evening—when you could sit and simply think about your day?
Donald:	Yeah, actually, every afternoon I usually go to the coffee shop and just sit and zone out with some coffee.
Counselor:	A good way to unwind? Is that something you do with your friends?

Donald:	Not usually. I like having some time by myself to listen to tunes, maybe scan the Internet or work on writing songs ... things like that.
Counselor:	That's super. Would it be possible, since you have your laptop, if maybe before you got too into your music, that you could think about your day and see if there was any time during the day that you found yourself getting angry or irritated?
Donald:	That's every day.
Counselor:	Well, maybe it would help if you could think of one time during the day that you were angry, just one, and then just jot a note to yourself about how angry you were during that time. You know, use a scale like of say 0 to 10, where 0 is like major mellow and not stressed, not irritated, and 10 almost becoming postal, like the worst anger you have ever had.
Donald:	Yeah, I could do that.
Counselor:	Well, could you also jot down a brief description of what was happening at the time—you know, what was going on? You don't have to write a lot, just enough so that when we get together you can look at your notes and really remember the situation.
Donald:	Like all the people and stuff going on?
Counselor:	Well, as much as you can—the more the better.
Donald:	Okay, I can try—like once a day?
Counselor:	That would be great, and obviously the more examples you can provide the better, but once a day would be super. Now that I have you on a roll, how about if after writing down a description of what was happening and how you were feeling, you take a moment and maybe reread what you wrote. But this time, try to pay attention to what is going through your mind as you think about the situation. You know how we talk to ourselves about these things? See if you can hear what you are thinking and just write whatever is going on in your mind. You don't have to worry about editing or anything, just write it down as it goes through your mind.
Donald:	That's kind of how I write my songs ... just like whatever comes to my mind I let go on the paper. So I could do that, but I'm not sure how this will help.
Counselor:	Well, I guess that is something we can decide when we look at what you wrote. My hope is that you may begin to see a pattern to your thinking and recognize certain types of thoughts that seem to be connected to your feelings of anger and irritation.
Donald:	Oh, that A-B-C stuff ... sure, I'm game.

While the counselor in Case Illustration 3.4 may have preferred that the student use a more formal, structured format such as the one in Figure 3.2, his reflections in practice led to allowance of a less structured form of data collection (journaling), at least as a starting point.

Helping students see the connection between their thinking to their feelings is sometimes made more difficult when students are unable to identify their evaluative thoughts actually occurring at the moment of upset. Part of the reason for this difficulty is there are cognitive assessments that occur at varying levels of consciousness. As you read the words on this page, you may also be aware of that internal voice that is directing you to "watch your time," or inviting you to "get something to eat" or even pondering "how much more will this guy drone on?" These thoughts that are readily available to your consciousness are sometimes referred to as "voluntary thoughts." However, some of these assessments, or interpretations, occur almost spontaneously and below the level of immediate awareness.

AUTOMATIC THOUGHTS

If we drill down or, if you prefer, go behind the surface, of voluntary thoughts we will find other less conscious and more rapid evaluations or automatic thoughts often exist. They are automatic, because they are not the result of an analysis of the problem; they are "knee-jerk" reactions to specific situations. And even though we may not be immediately aware of these automatic thoughts, since they happen so quickly and are so intricately and habitually connected to certain life events, they continue to color our experiences providing a unique tint of personal meaning.

Consider the situation where one awakes to the sight of newly fallen snow. For the second-grade student apprehensive about that day's school assignment, the snow is embraced as not simply something to view—to touch or to navigate through—but as a reprieve coming from on high and giving him one more day to breathe lightly. The thoughts the student may be able to identify with may be things such as, "Wow, it snowed!" or, "Mom, do we have school?" or even, "Can I go out?" However, these thoughts do not appear to immediately explain the sense of relief and actual euphoria the student is experiencing. If we are able to "drill down" under these thoughts we may unearth other more evaluative thoughts such as, "This is great—no tests, I won't fail today" or, "Whew, I didn't do my homework, and I'm off the hook." It is these thoughts which result in the dramatic sense of relief the student experiences, and yet they are thoughts that may not be readily accessible.

The following is one strategy that can be used to help a student understand the nature of automatic thoughts. With this technique, the counselor explains to the student that what is to follow is a little "experiment" used to demonstrate the existence of and affect of our automatic thoughts. The counselor would then show the student a colored marker and hold the marker as if it were some type of shooting instrument. Holding the marker at the student, the counselor would ask, "How would you feel if I stuck this pen out like this and said, 'stick em up'?" Most often, the student will respond by saying something like, " I don't know, I guess confused or a little silly," etc. Next the counselor would form his or her hand into the shape of a gun, point this symbolic gun at the student, and ask, "Now how would you feel if this (pointing to hand) was a real gun and I said 'stick em up'?" With this as the stimulus, most students will respond with statements reflecting anxiety, worry, or general concern. After completing these two simulations, the counselor explains that the student will be asked a question and should think about the question, and then answer it. The counselor explains to the student that the question is not a trick. Showing the student a colored marker and the hand formed as a symbolic gun again, the counselor says, "Look at these two things, and for this experiment, let's assume that this hand is really a gun, and of course this is a real marker. Now, here's the question I would like you to answer: 'What's the real difference between this marker and this gun?'"

Most students respond to this question by stating something indicating that the gun is dangerous and could hurt a person. While the response is most likely a true, accurate statement of what a gun can do, it is *not* the answer to the question the counselor asked. Perhaps, at this point you are confused; that would not be unusual and the student who is experiencing this "experiment" is most likely confused. To meet the confusion, the counselor should next hold the colored marker up and next to it a marker of a different color. Now the counselor will reintroduce the question, stating, "See these two markers? What are the real differences between them?" In this situation, the student will most likely look at the markers and then make comparisons of size, shape, and color of the markers. The student's noting apparent physical differences is an attempt to describe his or her perception of these stimuli at this moment in time. Contrast this to the first response when contrasting the hand-formed symbolic gun and the marker. In this case, rather than point out the differences in the perceived physical characteristics of two stimuli, for example size, shape, color and texture, the student responded by referring to a predicted use of the gun—that it could kill someone.

As noted, the prediction about possible use of a gun may be accurate, but it wasn't a response to the question posed. It wasn't the response the student gave when contrasting two markers. When asked to contrast the markers, the student likely did not predict how they could be used, saying something like, "Oh, that one writes in red and that one in black." Rather than responding with a prediction about their possible use, the student most likely simply described the here-and-now event. Why the difference in the student's response to the same questions? The difference is that when confronted with a gun, the student responded not from a voluntary thought level, but rather generated an automatic evaluative thought and it was that thought that served as the foundation for the student's response. As soon as the student saw the "gun," he or she jumped from a voluntary, conscious thought of, "That's a gun" to the underlying automatic thought such as, "Oh my god, this could kill me!" It is this latter thought that serves as the source of the student's emotional arousal and it is the thought that took form in the student's response.

In using this little experiment with a student, the counselor will note that the goal was not to suggest that the student's prediction is bad or invalid, but to simply demonstrate that some of the thoughts we have which affect our feelings and behaviors can occur below our immediate level of awareness. The counselor would want to help the student understand that once the thoughts affecting our feelings and behaviors can be identified, we will be able to test the validity of these thoughts and reframe and reformulate those that are unsupported and can cause us difficulty.

Identifying Automatic Thoughts

In helping the student identify his or her own automatic thoughts, the counselor would want to convey the directive, "Listen to your internal dialogue." While simply stated, such a prescription can be difficult to employ.

The counselor needs to highlight the fact that this process of identifying automatic thoughts is not easy. The student needs to be helped to see that these are nonreflective, brief presentations that have become somewhat habitual in certain situations and thus, like the response to the "gun," often occur without immediate awareness. The student could use a three-column thought log (see Figure 3.1) to begin to gather data for use in identifying these automatic thoughts. With this approach, the student would be asked to first describe in detail the event, and then as he or she reads or reflects on the event, to begin to simply record whatever thoughts can be identified. The student needs to be encouraged to write down any thought that he or she may have. The student needs to understand that it is okay if, initially, all that can be written are thoughts such as, "I can't think of anything" or "This is silly." But in session or as homework, the student would be prompted to reread the description of the situation or event, and while doing so, ask questions such as: "What does the event mean?" "So, what do I think will happen?" "What does this suggest about me? About others?" The use of such probing questions may help the student move beyond the listing of immediate voluntary thoughts to unearth the underlying evaluative meaning that serves as the source of the feelings of concern.

SCHEMA AND FUNDAMENTAL BELIEFS

As the counselor and student review the thought logs, consistent themes may emerge in reference to personal evaluation (e.g., I'm just a loser, failure, or worthless); views of others (e.g., no one likes me, or everybody is stupid); or perspectives on the world as a whole (e.g., it's too dangerous out there). These themes reflect the student's fundamental beliefs and they give shape to the student's reactions to a wide variety of situations. These core beliefs develop from early childhood and while they may have served the student well in making sense of his or her world when very young, it may never have occurred to the student to evaluate whether the beliefs are the most useful ways of understanding his or her school-aged experiences.

Identifying Fundamental Core Beliefs/Schemata

As with the automatic thoughts, core beliefs may be identified if the student can be helped to question what the initial thoughts suggest about his or her overall view of "self" or worldview and his or her future. Attempting to have the student identify exactly what is anticipated, and what it means if the thoughts were true, may help to unearth this guiding set of underlying assumptions that color much of the student's lived experience. The process is illustrated in the following brief exchange.

Counselor: Walt, maybe you could help me out. Look here (pointing to an entry on the thought log). You wrote down that you were looking at a picture of Ellie and became very upset. You apparently were so upset that you wrote down you were depressed at a 95 percent level.

Walt: Yeah, it was horrible. I just stayed in my room and I think I cried myself to sleep.

Counselor: I'm sorry to hear that, but I'm wondering, while it is clear it is not easy to have a relationship end, especially if it was something you really enjoyed, I am not quite sure what the event means to you. You did a great job writing down your thoughts and I see you wrote down, "Ellie broke up with me." But what does that mean? She broke up with you?

Walt: I must be a loser?

Counselor: Well, I'm not sure of that connection, but let's stay with that thought. So, what would it mean if you were a loser?

Walt: Are you kidding? I would never have anyone in my life . . . I'll be alone for the rest of my life.

Counselor: And if that were true, what would that say about you?

Walt: I'm a real crap. No one could want me. I'm unlovable.

What is clear from the above brief exchange is that Walt is using one experience of rejection as evidence that he is rejectable and unlovable. It appears he has developed a fundamental core belief that he must be loved by all in order to be lovable, and the rejection in this relationship forces him to assume the alternative—that he is not lovable and will thus spend his life alone. Without dismissing the pain this student is experiencing, the counselor in this situation needs to sensitively challenge Walt's underlying assumption that he needs to be liked and approved of by virtually everyone to be lovable and valuable.

ADAPTING A COGNITIVE APPROACH FOR YOUNGER STUDENTS

While strategies such as journaling or using the A-B-C log may prove useful for many of our students, more active, hands-on strategies may prove more effective for those children who are preschool or in early education. Friedberg and McClure (2004) suggest that when working with younger students, counselors choose active, fun tasks that are developmentally sensitive and appealing. To this end, the counselor employing a cognitive orientation may use workbooks, stories, props, colorful drawings, and hands-on activities to facilitate the student's understanding of the thought-feeling connection and the identification of automatic thoughts.

Workbooks

The benefit of using workbooks with our students is that they provide concrete activities to help teach the student the somewhat abstract principles of cognitive counseling (Kendall, 1988, 1990; Vernon, 1989). For example, Kendall's (1990) *Coping Cat Workbook* provides an illustration of two cats each having a different image of the same sleeping dog. The young student is shown one cat that "sees" the dog as menacing and threatening, and a second cat that perceives the dog as a harmless canine.

The image provides a concrete illustration of the thought-feeling connection, one easily grasped by even the youngest student and one that provides a meaningful reference point for the counselor-student dialogue.

Incorporating Play and Student Interests

Play, including structured board games, provides a useful option for the cognitively oriented school counselor while facilitating the student's understanding of the power of thought to feeling (Knell, 1998). The game format provides the stimulus and structure needed to elicit student responses that can then be processed in session as illustrations of the thought-feeling connection. In one such game (see Berg, 1990), a game card presents a situation in which a girl is criticized by her mother and has negative automatic thoughts such as, "I look dumb. Everybody will laugh at me." In playing the game, the student would be asked to identify the negative, automatic thought being illustrated, and then asked to replace it with a more adaptive self-statement. The specific structure of the game not only provides the counselor a "teaching" opportunity, but the young student's style of responding to even this stimulus question may provide the school counselor with a real here-and-now experience to process with the child. For example, if the child responds to the card with angry comments ("This is dumb"), the astute school counselor can use this response in light of the situation as material to process an illustration of the thinking-feeling connection.

The various game prompts provide the opportunity to directly teach the student the specific cognitive principles, however it is in guiding the student to see personal application that the real "counseling" occurs. For example, a counselor working with a young preschool student who becomes overwhelmingly anxious at the thought of standing up in the front of the room to share something during "show and tell" may tell or read a story such as *The Little Engine That Could* (Piper, 1976). This could help the student not only see the connection of this fictional situation to his or her own, but also help the student embrace and employ a self-talk strategy such as repeating the phrase, "I think I can" along with the image of the little engine being strong and successful to overcome the fear of public speaking.

Another strategy is for the counselor to incorporate the student's interests and preferred activities into each session as the materials to employ in teaching the fundamental cognitive principles. Relating the principles to the student's interests helps make the principles clear, concrete, and personal. For example, the counselor working with a first-grade student who was exhibiting social anxiety decided to use baseball as the context to present the thought-feeling connection.

Counselor: Bernard, so the Phillies are your favorite baseball team?

Bernard: Yeah.

Counselor: Do you have a favorite player on the team?

Bernard: I like Chase Utley. He plays second base like me.

Counselor: Wow. So you play second base, too. That's neat. You know, I always wondered about something.

Bernard: Huh?

Counselor: Well, sometimes the team is down to their last out and they need one more hit to win the game. I just wonder how guys like Chase Utley can get up to bat and be calm and focused, with all those screaming fans. What do you think he is thinking about when he goes to bat?

Bernard: I don't know. My coach always tells us to relax our hands and keep our eye on the ball.

Counselor: I bet that's the kind of thing Chase thinks about. I wonder what would happen if he stood at the plate and started to think, "Oh, my gosh. Everybody is looking at me. If I make an out the team will hate me."

Bernard: I bet he would be scared that he was going to make an out.

Counselor: I think you are right. If he thinks something bad will happen, he will get really nervous, really scared, but if he keeps thinking about the ball and his hands being relaxed then he is relaxed. I wonder if thinking like Chase Utley might help you at those times when you think you are going to mess up and everybody will be angry with you?

The counselor in this situation not only introduces Bernard to the idea of the "thought-feeling" connection, but also lays the foundation for a problem-solving technique that Bernard can use when at bat or in those situations when he feels overly concerned about other people's reactions. This is an example of the counselor embedding the cognitive principles within the student's preferred activities.

Other activities, such as using puppets or small dolls as "players" in a self-dialogue scenario or employing role play with the counselor as self-talk, are approaches that can help the younger students grasp the thought-feeling connection. The creative use of cartoons or even stick figures with "thought bubbles" used to amplify the character's thinking may be a useful strategy for introducing the younger student to the thought-feeling connection. With this approach, the counselor could even use the prompt "thought bubble" as a way to invite the student to become aware of what he or she is thinking at any one time.

For the school counselor working with the younger student, it is essential that the opportunities and limitations presented, given the student's developmental level, are appreciated. It is also essential for the school counselor to possess the knowledge and skills necessary to translate the cognitive principles into teachable experience.

Additional resources for working with younger students are presented at the end of Chapter 5.

WHAT'S NEXT?

Helping our students understand the thought-feeling connection is but the first target for our counseling. Once this connection is understood and embraced, the school counselor and student, working in collaboration, will now begin to review the specific thoughts held by the student and assess the degree to which these thoughts accurately reflect the reality of the events, and provide a base for functional and adaptive feelings and behaviors.

SUMMARY

Cognitions as Mediators of Feelings and Actions

The school counselor employing a cognitive-orienting framework maintains that the way an individual evaluates situations or events is the primary determiner of affect and behavior.

An Idea Difficult to Embrace

While it is relatively easy to provide case illustrations to highlight the role of thoughts as mediators between events and emotional and behavioral consequences, it is not that easy to "convince" students that the source of their pain, their upset, is truly themselves and not the external conditions in which they find themselves.

Promoting Understanding of the Importance of Cognition

Helping a student understand the centrality of thinking to feeling is truly a challenge for the school counselor operating with a cognitive

(Continued)

(Continued)

orientation. There are no simple or singular approaches to accomplish this task. The following are strategies presented within this chapter.

- View events from multiple perspectives—a simple "test."
- Choose the feeling by choosing the thought.
- Use a three-column approach (in search of monsters).

From Theory to Personal Application

Understanding the principle of thought as mediator to feelings and behaviors is one thing, owning it and seeing its application to one's lived experience is quite another.

Having the student gather data on his or her own experiences and "analyze" those experiences, in light of the specific interpretations provided by the student, facilitates this personal ownership.

Automatic Thoughts and Schema

Cognitive assessments occur at varying levels of consciousness— voluntary, automatic, and core beliefs.

- Voluntary thoughts are readily available to our consciousness.
- Automatic thoughts are less conscious and more rapid evaluations of life experiences.
- Schema and fundamental beliefs are revealed as the counselor and student review the thought logs, and consistent themes subsequently emerge in reference to personal evaluation (e.g., I'm just a loser, failure, or worthless); views of others (e.g., no one likes me, or everybody is stupid); or perspectives on the world as a whole (e.g., it's too dangerous out there). These themes reflect the student's fundamental beliefs and they give shape to the student's reactions to a wide variety of situations.

Adaptation for Younger Students

While strategies such as journaling or using the A-B-C log may prove useful for many of our students, more active, hands-on strategies may prove more effective for preschoolers or children in early education.

The counselor employing a cognitive orientation may use workbooks, stories, props, colorful drawings, and hands-on activities to facilitate the student's understanding of the thought-feeling connection and the identification of automatic thoughts.

Identifying Cognitive Distortions

4

"I'm telling you, she hates me. They all hate me. I know that these teachers talk behind my back and they all want me out. It's just like my other school. They plotted against me and it's happening again."

—Marcy, age 10

The school counselor confronted by a student who firmly believes that her failing grades are the result of the entire faculty plotting in an elaborate plan to have her removed from school would clearly be concerned about this student's grasp on reality. It would seem obvious to most of those observing this response that it was disproportionate to the actual event (failing a couple of courses) and clearly misperceiving the intentions of the counselor and those teachers expressing concern. In this situation, the student's distorted interpretations and distortion of reality are clear. But how about the student who presents in the counselor's office totally distraught because his parents won't allow him to have a cell phone, or the student who is furious because another student took his seat on the bus? Would the school counselor see these students as radically and dramatically distorting reality? Would the school counselor identify the students' emotional responses as evidence of their distorted thinking? Or, would most adults, and many counselors, simply write them off as a normal, or at least "typical" developmental phenomenon, one requiring little to no counseling?

Whether these latter forms of dysfunctional thinking appear developmentally normative or "typical," they are nevertheless distortions of reality and they result in very upsetting and disruptive feelings and behaviors. Further, even though the student may see the "truth" and "logic" in his or her thinking, it is a "logic" that is the source of the student's upset and thus needs to be challenged and reformulated.

Once the school counselor feels that the student has begun to embrace the connection of thoughts to feelings (see Chapter 3), attention is turned to the identification of, and challenge to, the student's cognitive distortions. During this stage of the counseling, the school counselor will develop and implement strategies to help the student understand the nature of cognitive distortions, and then learn to identify specific dysfunctional processing and cognitive distortions that serve as the source of the current emotional upset and concerns.

A PROCESS REQUIRING SENSITIVITY

It is tempting to take a somewhat academic approach to the issue of recognizing and confronting cognitive distortions. It is a relative easy task to develop a working definition of a cognitive distortion, and then apply criteria to test the "rationality" of the thoughts presented. However, it is essential for the counselor to remember that these private thoughts have served as this student's reality for some time.

Regardless of how silly or far-fetched a student's thoughts may appear to the counselor, it must be remembered that these seem reasonable to the student. The effective counselor will approach this process understanding that the student's thoughts are, at the moment, his or her reality and it is a reality, while painful, that is hard to surrender given the personal validity assigned to those beliefs.

Consider the experience of the three- or four-year-old child who hides under his covers, truly terrified by the belief that there is a monster in his room. As adults, we can rapidly process the reality that this child is taking an event, such as a squeaky floor or branch at the window, and distorting that reality to make it into an extremely threatening, and monstrous experience. The sad result of this distortion is the child's experience of real terror. And even though we recognize the distorted thinking causing such upset, we are also fully cognizant that the intense fear and terror experienced by the child is *real* and, as such, we would approach the child with the sensitivity, comfort, and support required of one so terrified. Similarly, it would be easy to simply dismiss the student whose whole world has collapsed because she wasn't invited to the third-grade birthday party, or the student who is depressed over not being chosen as the lead in the school play, as being too dramatic. But as empathic school counselors, we respect the pain the students are experiencing and thus find ways to gently and respectfully confront distortions in the students' thinking causing such upset.

And while confronting distortions seems to be a relatively straight-forward intervention, the school counselor needs to remember that these beliefs—even though clearly dysfunctional—are not easily surrendered, nor most likely even recognized by the student as "dysfunctional." As noted previously, when experiencing nonconfirming information, the student may actually reshape that information, that experience, in order to fit or assimilate it into the existing, even dysfunctional, schema, rather than change that schema. The following brief exchange illustrates one student's stance in defense of his distorted self-percept. The student, Lawrence, was referred to counseling by his English teacher who felt that he was simply not living up to his potential in her class. On preliminary investigation, the counselor discovered that Lawrence had previously been an A student but since the beginning of semester, his teachers have noted a drop in his academic performance. The exchange that follows took place in mid-session.

Counselor: Well, Lawrence, as I listen to you describe all the things that you are, as you say, "messin' up," it seems to me that you are really building quite a case to support your idea that you really are a failure?

Lawrence: I'm not building a case . . . I'm just stating the facts. Look, I am failing school and probably won't graduate, my SATs really suck, sorry, and I got cut from baseball. That's just the way it is.

Counselor: But there's where I'm confused. I know you are failing both math and English for this marking period, but you still have a passing grade in both classes for the year, and I just saw that you received two letters of college acceptance.

Lawrence: Yeah right (sarcastically and ignoring the evidence of pass-ing and even being accepted to college). Both schools will accept anyone; it's like open door U for losers. There's no way in hell I'm getting in to a good school.

The counselor employing a cognitive-orienting framework appreciates that a student such as Lawrence truly does not wish to hold on to these beliefs that have caused him so much pain. However, the reality is that he continues to embrace these thoughts, these damaging beliefs, because they "appear" to him to be accurate, valid reflections of his reality. Further, since we are wired to retain our beliefs, even in the face of contradictory information, Lawrence is quick to ignore the contradictory information regarding his college acceptance and general academic standings. The task for the counselor is to not only identify information that is contradictory to the student's dysfunctional schema, but then creatively, sensitively, and, most importantly, effectively present these data in ways that make the student unable to escape recognizing the degree to which these thoughts are distortions. Once the student begins to recognize his or her dysfunctional thoughts, he or she will be helped in challenging and reformulating these dysfunctional beliefs so they are more accurate reflections of reality, and result in more successful adaptation to the issues at hand. This step in a cognitive-counseling model is more fully described in Chapter 5.

IRRATIONAL BELIEFS

As the target of this second "phase" of the counseling, the school counselor with a cognitive orientation will attempt to educate the student about the nature of irrational and dysfunctional thinking. In working with the student, the counselor may ask the student to consider each of the following questions as they address specific characteristics of rational thinking.

1. Rational thinking is consistent with known facts: "Are my thinking and beliefs consistent with known facts and reality?"

2. Rational thinking helps one adapt and function the way one desires, promoting moderate emotions or emotions that move an individual in a desired direction, facilitating goal attainment: "Are my thinking and beliefs helping or hindering me over the long run?"

3. Rational thinking makes sense and is logical: "Are my thinking and beliefs logical?"

While the school counselor may not literally teach these criteria to the student, he or she will use them to help point out the error of the student's thinking or question the validity of the student's thoughts. This is a step toward educating the student to recognize those ill-founded thoughts serving as the source of the concern. Consider the situation where two students come to the counselor's office anxious about the upcoming final exam. The first student expresses concerns that she *may not* do so well on the exam, and that *if* she messes the exam up, it *could* lower her grade in this one course. The student's thoughts are framed as possibilities, not absolutes, and the worst-case scenario projected—that is, getting a lower grade in this one course—results in a moderate level of anxiety. Further, this anxiety appears useful in that it serves as a motivation for the student to choose to stay in over the weekend, studying, rather than going out with her friends. In this situation, the possibility of not doing well is reality-based and the conclusion that it would lower her overall grade is factual. Further, the level of anxiety created by this evaluative thought resulted in the student taking adaptive action with a focused goal. Under these conditions, it would appear that this student's thoughts are rational and functional.

Contrast this to our second student who comes to the counselor's office in a state of total panic. The student explains that she has a major exam coming up that she's *going* to fail, and as a result *will fail* the course, and as such, "*will blow her chances of ever getting into college!*" In this situation, the level of anxiety created by the belief that she will fail and that this failure will ultimately result in her never, ever, getting into college is certainly not factual. The anxiety that results from such catastrophic thinking is at such a level that it interferes with any action the student may want to take to increase the likelihood of her success on the test. The student has difficulty concentrating, is unable to sit still and organize her materials, and finds that her ability to remember and retrieve information for the test is blocked by the anxiety. If one were to apply the previously described criteria for rational or irrational thinking, it is clear that our second student's thoughts are irrational and result in levels of anxiety and behaviors that are dysfunctional as a mechanisms to help her achieve her goal of passing the test.

Common Irrational Beliefs

When working with school-aged children, it is not unusual to find their irrational or dysfunctional thinking to be clustered into one of the following categories. The listing is neither exhaustive nor reflective of every child the school counselor may encounter. However, the following descriptions can serve as a framework for further understanding and identifying a student's dysfunctional thinking.

Personal Identity and Worth

The first framework surrounds thoughts reflecting issues of personal identity and self-worth. Most counselors have experienced the somewhat exhausting and elaborate strategies our students employ to be accepted and part of an "in" crowd. Wanting to belong and have a group of close, supportive friends is healthy and desirable. However, for some students, the issue of being accepted is not merely an issue of social belonging. Rather, it is elevated to a level that defines personal worth and value.

It is not unusual for some children and adolescents to believe that it is essential to be liked by most, if not all, of the people they identify as significant in their lives. With this as an operative assumption, these students are likely to do everything and anything that is needed to get the approval they crave. Sadly, with this as a fundamental core belief, the student may engage in numerous self-damaging behaviors, including drug and alcohol use, promiscuous sex, or even willful academic failure—all in order just to "fit in" and be accepted. Further, when this affirmation is not immediately evident, it is not unusual for a student with this operative assumption to fall into a state of depression, seeing this lack of approval as evidence of his or her own personal worthlessness.

Often, students operating from this mandate to be "approved of by all" feel as if they need to be completely competent and perfect in order to be accepted. Certainly, students embracing such thinking will find themselves experiencing and exhibiting extreme anxiety in situations where they feel they may be evaluated. Similarly, those students who hold the core belief that a person needs to be perfectly competent to be successful and acceptable may find themselves needlessly obsessing about minor details, or conversely, choosing to withdraw from tasks with which they are clearly competent to complete for fear of having less than perfect results.

From "I Want" to "I Must Have"

A second group of irrational beliefs often exhibited by students involve a rigid sense of getting what they want. Rather than seeing the acquisition of desired things or the engagement in desired activities as something that is nice and preferable, students with this core belief often perceive getting what they want as an absolute must—a have to—and an essential element of life. While this may sound dramatic, the belief is real to those students who hold it and the consequence of not filling that "need" is experienced as devastating.

With such an orientation and a sense of "essentialness," these students will exhibit panic, anger, hostility, and jealousy when not receiving what they believe to be what they absolutely must have. While the school counselor may be able to relate to a person in a panic state because the person is not getting the flow of oxygen needed to survive, it may be more difficult to appreciate that a similar sense of panic is experienced when one fails to be chosen for the lead in the school play. The students who show explosive behavior in response to a rejection of a request to be taken to the mall, or failure to get the grade that they "know" they deserve, truly see these situations as horrible, unbearable, and catastrophic rather than merely disappointing. These students often react with uncontrollable anger in response to what is firmly believed as a major injustice, or may respond with panic believing that an essential part of his or her life has been denied.

No Bumps in the Road of Life

The final set of fundamental beliefs often exhibited by our students is that life should be fun and comfortable at all times, a bump-free road of life. Students with this perspective experience normal frustrations, disappointment, and difficulties as intolerable. Often these students avoid engaging in challenging schoolwork or hesitate to take risks that venture out of their comfort zones. These are the students that invest energy in taking the least challenging path rather than the path that will lead to the most growth and productivity, and when encountering "bumps" along the way, often respond with near hysteria.

It is not simply the type of thought or cluster of thoughts that may be dysfunctional. For some students, the actual cognitive processes used to draw conclusions may be distorted and, as such, result in dysfunctional feeling and behaviors.

COGNITIVE DISTORTIONS

Most school counselors have encountered students who take a single event and overgeneralize to their entire life and future. Or perhaps it's the students who personalize events concluding that this or that only happens to them. In either situation, the student distorts the events and draws erroneous conclusions. These students may, for example, selectively abstract some data from the pool available while dismissing or discounting some other essential information as they draw their conclusions about life, self, and the world. Cognitive processes such as overgeneralization, personalization, and selective abstraction create a distorted view of the student's reality and result in dysfunctional feelings and behaviors.

At this stage of counseling, the school counselor operating with a cognitive orientation will want to educate the student on the nature of cognitive distortions and their impact. David Burns (1999) has provided an insightful look at the issue and impact of cognitive distortions. A modification of his description of a number of the more common forms of cognitive distortion is presented in this section. In reviewing the various forms of distortions, two points may become clear. First, there is a very good chance that all of us have employed one or many of these distortions to process an experience or an event in our own lives. The very fact that cognitive distortions may be statistically normative in our culture is not evidence that they are desirable or functional. The second point is that often the students you council may use multiple distortions to process any one specific event.

Selective Abstraction or Filtering

Often when presented with a situation offering many pieces of information and data, we focus on only some of these data, ignoring the rest. The student who selectively abstracts just some information from all the information surrounding a particular event targets a single data point, or group of data, as the lens to interpret the situation, even though there are multiple pieces of information which conflict with this interpretation. Consider the student who is very depressed and describes a situation where he and a friend from the school band were made fun of at lunch for being band "nerds." The student explains that it was horrible and everybody was laughing, and he and his friend had to go sit with the other band members. Using this experience, the student selects only evidence of rejection to form the conclusion that "no one likes him," and that he is a loser. It would appear that this conclusion is the result of filtering "in" only those data that support such a position (i.e., these students mocked him) while filtering out the conflicting data such as the fact that he came to lunch with a friend, others at lunch were not laughing, and he was able to rejoin a group (the band members) for lunch.

If all data were included as the basis from which to draw conclusions, this student would have most likely concluded that while some kids certainly make fun of band members, that he, regardless, has numerous friends who show concern and support for him and thus provide evidence that he is valued and not a loser.

Dichotomous or Black and White Thinking

A student employing dichotomous, or black and white thinking, holds rigidly to a "this or that," "either/or," "right or wrong" approach to life. For this student, people and things are seen as good or bad, wonderful or horrible, desirable or intolerable. There is little room for the "in between."

With this orientation, the student does not allow room for human error or being less than perfect, whether this is in reference to self or others. Rather than seeing error as part of the human experience, the student sees this error as evidence of failure to be perfect and thus, with a black and white orientation, concludes that he or she is perfectly imperfect. Students with this particular orientation will respond to a single experience of failure or rejection as if these are evidence for being "failures" and "rejectable." With such an orientation, these students may become despondent, no longer engage in these activities, or withdraw from social contact since they "know" that it is, and they are, absolutely hopeless.

Magnifying and Minimizing

For some students, a minor mistake, small setback, or criticism is processed as a huge, life-altering event. With magnification as a cognitive-processing error, small mistakes become tragic failures, a minor criticism becomes a total rejection, and simple setbacks now seem like unconquerable hurdles.

The use of magnification may often be accompanied by an equally destructive process of minimizing small personal achievements or evidence of support since these data conflict with the perceived magnification of the situation. Thus the student, while holding five letters of acceptance to quality universities, finds herself absorbed by the one letter of rejection and she used this one to conclude that she will never be able to amount to anything in life.

Catastrophizing

Students for whom the process of magnification has become a cognitive style of life view all of life's challenges or problems as major unsolvable catastrophes, rather simply problems to be resolved. When confronted with disappointments or problems, a student with this orientation believes that these are both unsolvable and, at the same time, intolerable. For these students, headaches are responded to as if they are brain tumors, a single bad grade is embraced as the end of all possible career choices, a mistake in front of others is perceived as the basis for total social rejection, and the experience of loss is embraced as an intolerable event that will forever remove all experiences of joy from their lives. Sadly elevating life problems, regardless of their "real" severity, to the level of catastrophe makes the problems truly unsolvable and thus immobilizes the student in any effort to resolve the issue of concern.

Overgeneralizing

With this form of cognitive distortion, a student will tend to draw broad, sweeping conclusions based on a single experience. For example, a student with this orientation may take a situation such as striking out during a baseball game as evidence that not only will he never get a hit, but that this one event is evidence that he is completely incompetent in many domains. Similarly, a student employing overgeneralization may take the experience of being turned down when asking another to the dance as the basis from which to conclude, "No one would ever go to a dance with me" and, as such, retreats as a social isolate.

The student processing through the distorted lens of overgeneralization frames his or her experience using words such as "none," "every," "always," and "never," as well as descriptors such as "the worst," "a waste," and "absolute jerks." While there may be some grain of truth buried within the judgment, the student ignores all contrary evidence and modulating information.

Personalizing

Developmental theory and research would suggest that school-aged children and adolescents often exhibit cognitive orientations best described as egocentric. For many students, life is truly "all about them." But beyond this developmental artifact, some students engage in somewhat extreme egocentric thinking, employing the cognitive distortion of personalization as a response to a life event.

Students employing personalization often take responsibility for events (most often negative events) for which they have had no primary responsibility. The young student who is anxious believing that his angry thoughts caused his father's illness, or the adolescent whose parents wouldn't be getting a divorce if she only did better in school, are both employing this cognitive distortion.

As may be apparent from the two illustrations, one sad consequence of this personalization is that students can carry intense and debilitating guilt about things over which they had little control, or feel extreme anxiety about "responsibilities" that they truly do not own nor have the power to impact.

Asserting Shoulds and Musts

Most of us employ terms such as "should" and "must" in describing our actions. For example, we might state, "I should really exercise," or "I must remember to pay the bills," or "I shouldn't eat the piece of cake." The use of these words is in and of itself innocuous if, that is, we use the words to simply reflect our desires, our wants, and our wishes. However, oftentimes these terms reflect not merely our desire for a preferred action or experience, but reflect our very rigid, inflexible view of the way we believe that we, and the world, absolutely must be.

Consider the student who goes ballistic when given a detention for talking during a fire drill. This student is quick to defend his actions, noting, "It was just a stupid drill," "I had to ask about an assignment," and "It was only one question," etc. The student's response indicates that from his perspective the rules of this world (i.e., no talking when practicing a fire drill) are simply not acceptable and therefore it is totally unjust for him to be punished for violating such inane rules.

The issue here isn't whether or not the rule makes sense. The reality is that the world (in this case the school) is the way it is regardless of how we feel it must be. Further, firmly and rigidly believing that it has to be as we define it to be is irrational and results in dysfunctional feelings and behaviors. The young child who has planned for days for a family trip to the zoo might be thrown in an uncontrollable rage, or tantrum, if severe thunderstorms necessitate canceling the trip. For this child, the belief that it is absolutely unacceptable and that "you promised," meaning that he *must* go regardless, results not just in the emotional outburst but quite likely behavior that further brings negative consequences. The child who could see the thunderstorm as merely an unfortunate event, one which is disappointing, would be sad but most likely be able to adapt in order to make the best out of a rainy day.

This is not to suggest one shouldn't develop a set of personal standards and values to guide decision making. It is valuable to set personal standards to guide our decisions and our behaviors; however, we need to remember that they are *our* standards. These standards or "personal laws" of how we wish to be, or how we hope the world will be, apply only to us and truly cannot be expected to be embraced by the world at large. When this set of personal standards becomes inflexible—standards that we believe are universally applicable—then they will result in nonadaptive and disruptive feelings and actions.

Thus, in the case of the student "fire-drill talker," rather than effectively working to change a rule perceived as unneeded or nonuseful, the student's rigid belief ("this simply could not be this way, and therefore *must* be different") resulted in his violation of the rule, his angry reaction when sanctioned, and his appearance in detention—all things which seem to have been counterproductive.

IDENTIFYING PERSONAL DISTORTIONS

While the goal at this point of the counseling is to assist the student to understand the concept of cognitive distortion, it is not merely an academic goal. There are no tests to be taken nor is it really essential that the student be able to make fine distinction between the various types of cognitive distortions. The goal in reviewing these various forms of distortion is to help the student understand that he or she, and we, can and do distort reality. Further, the counselor at this point wants to demonstrate that the conclusions we draw using such faulty cognitive processes result in nonadaptive, dysfunctional feelings and behaviors.

In helping the student begin to understand the impact of such cognitive distortions on feelings and actions, the school counselor may employ a variety of directive, didactic teaching methods. The counselor could prepare written descriptions or illustrations of each of the distortions and give these to the student as a way to help the student understand the various forms and nature of cognitive distortions (see Table 4.1). The counselor could present sample scenarios, or even role-play, to allow the student to see each of these particular forms of distortion in action along with the resulting feelings and behaviors.

Table 4.1   Cognitive Distortions

All-or-Nothing Thinking: A person sees things as only black or white. If someone points out that this individual made a mistake, he or she is thus less than perfect, and sees self as a total failure.
Overgeneralizing: A person takes a single negative event and concludes that all others will be the same. This individual may conclude that, if he or she invites one person out and is rejected, then all people will reject this person if subsequent invites are made.
Mental Filtering: A person pulls out only the bad events in his or her life, overlooking the positives. There is a filter that allows some things (negative details) in and excludes any contradictory, positive information. The result is that the person's view of all reality becomes negative.
Disqualifying the Positive: A person rejects positive experiences, finding reasons to simply dismiss or discount these positives. This is the process that allows one to hold on to negative beliefs when contradicted by a positive experience.
Jumping to Conclusions: A person makes a negative interpretation even though there are no definite facts that convincingly support this conclusion. This is what leads a person to not want to bother, "knowing" he or she will fail, be rejected, or not get the position, etc. without even attempting the task at hand.
Magnification (Catastrophizing) or Minimizing: A person either exaggerates the importance of things (such as a goof-up or someone else's achievement), or reduces something like a positive personal trait until it appears tiny and perhaps relatively meaningless.
Emotional Reasoning: A person uses emotions, or feelings, as a basis to draw conclusions about reality. Someone may experience anxiety and conclude that there must be something dangerous happening, or could feel overwhelmed by a work assignment, and conclude that it is therefore hopeless and will never be completed.
Personalizing: A person takes responsibility for events (most often negative events) for which he or she has had no primary responsibility.

In addition to helping the student grasp the concept of cognitive distortion, the counselor wants to assist the student in identifying those distortions that appear to be occurring within his or her own thinking. As such, the school counselor will encourage the student to continue to gather data on his or her own thoughts and resulting feelings. These data can be brought to counseling for discussion and analysis.

The school counselor using a cognitive orientation will review the student's data (i.e., thought log) and, with well-timed and carefully phrased questions, challenge the student's conclusions and invite alternative ways of "seeing" the event. For example, consider the effectiveness of the questioning posed by the counselor in the following case. The interaction occurred during a session with a sixteen-year-old girl, Maura, who was feeling extreme guilt and despondency because of her "sinfulness." The counselor had previously identified that the client's sense of guilt was supported by her "friend," Louise, who commented that Maura's "making out" with a boy was damnable.

Counselor: So, Maura, if I understand correctly, you feel so "sinful" because you made out with a boy after the dance?

Maura: Well, it was more than that. This was the church dance and we had youth group right before, and they told us how we should avoid the sins of the flesh . . . and here I go . . . and get into it.

Counselor: So, "getting into it," means making out?

Maura: Yes, that's all I did, but when I told Louise, she told me that I was immoral and sinful, and that I was giving into the sins of the flesh and clearly not loving of Jesus, my Lord and savior . . . this is unforgivable!

Counselor: Maura, I know you and your family are very much involved with your church, but I'm a little confused. I mean, if Louise were here sitting on your left hand side, saying to you, "You are a sinner. You have committed an unforgivable sin by making out with this boy," how would you feel?

Maura: Well, that's what she said, and I believe her. I feel scared I'm going to go to hell.

Counselor: I'm sure that's upsetting, but here's my confusion. Let's pretend that Louise is here saying these things, but on your right side, let's pretend that Jesus is sitting there—and if I understand your faith—you feel that Jesus is the son of God and that Jesus chose to die for you because of his love for you? So what do you think Jesus would say about you making out with this boy?

Maura: He would say that I shouldn't do that (beginning to cry)!

Counselor: Perhaps. But what might he say about you going to hell?

Maura: No, he would say he loves me and that he forgave me and that I need to be careful about my worldly desires.

Counselor: So, I guess I am not sure whom you want to listen to . . . Louise? Or Jesus?

Maura: I guess Louise (smiling) . . . is wrong?

While the counselor was able to employ his own understanding of the student's orienting framework (i.e., Christian theology), it was the gentle questioning that opened the student's thinking about the issue of her "sinfulness" in a way that allowed her to challenge her initial beliefs and reframe the situation in a way that would be more adaptive and functional to living life as she wishes.

School counselors with a cognitive orientation will use a variety of techniques to confront and dispute their students' distorted cognitions, but as illustrated with Louise, the creative use of questions and a Socratic style may be one of the most effective strategies.

WORKING WITH YOUNGER STUDENTS

Cognitive principles, including the identification of cognitive distortions, and later, the reeducation and reformulation of belief systems (see Chapter 5), can be employed by school counselors working with younger students. In employing these principles, the counselor needs to be aware of and sensitive to the developmental limitations being presented.

For example, while direct confrontation of irrational and distorted cognitions may prove effective for the preadolescent and adolescent, there is a chance that the younger student may perceive this confrontation as scolding or as evidence of the counselor's rejection. Less direct approaches to the identification of irrational beliefs and cognitive distortions may elicit less resistance and allow the student to process and embrace the principle being illustrated.

Because younger students respond better to concrete counselors, the use of stories, songs, games, worksheets, and even role playing will be effective strategies to convey the principles underlying counseling from a cognitive perspective. For example, children can be told stories illustrating how two different students, perhaps twins, encountered the same event but reacted differently because of the unique way each one interpreted the situation. Readers interested in further strategies adaptable to the younger student may want to consult the additional resources listed at the end of Chapter 5.

SUMMARY

**Identifying Cognitive Distortions:
A Process Requiring Sensitivity**

- Regardless of how silly or far-fetched a student's thoughts may appear to the counselor, it must be remembered that these seem reasonable to the student. These private thoughts have served as this student's reality for some time.
- When experiencing nonconfirming information, the student may actually reshape that information, that experience, in order to fit or assimilate it into the existing, even dysfunctional, schema, rather than change that schema.
- The task for the counselor is to not only identify information that is contradictory to the student's dysfunctional schema, but to then creatively, sensitively, and most importantly, effectively present these data in ways so that the student is unable to escape recognizing the degree to which these thoughts are distortions.

Irrational and Rational Beliefs

- Rational thinking is consistent with known facts: "Are my thinking and beliefs consistent with known facts and reality?"
- Rational thinking helps one adapt and function the way one desires, promoting emotions that move an individual in a desired direction, facilitating goal attainment: "Are my thinking and beliefs helping or hindering me in the long-run?"
- Rational thinking makes sense and is logical: "Are my thinking and beliefs logical?"
- Common irrational beliefs presented by school-aged children involve themes of personal identity and worth, confusing wants with absolute musts and needs, and demands for life to be fun and comfortable at all times.

(Continued)

(Continued)

Cognitive Distortions

Not only can the specific thought be irrational, but also the actual process used to process data may be distorted. Typical forms of cognitive distortion include:

- selective abstraction or filtering
- dichotomous or black and white thinking
- magnifiying and minimizing
- catastrophizing
- overgeneralizating
- personalizing
- asserting should or musts

Identifying Personal Distortions

- In helping the student begin to understand the impact of such cognitive distortions on feelings and actions, the school counselor may employ a variety of directive, didactic teaching methods, including presenting prepared written descriptions or illustrations of each of the distortions.

Working With Younger Students

- In employing these principles, the counselor needs to be aware of and sensitive to the developmental limitations being presented. For example, while direct confrontation of irrational and distorted cognitions may prove effective for the preadolescent and adolescent, there is a chance that the younger student may perceive this confrontation as a scolding or as evidence of the counselor's rejection.
- Because younger students respond better to concrete counselors, effective strategies for working with these students include stories, songs, games, worksheets, and even role play to convey the principles underlying counseling from a cognitive perspective.

Reformulating Dysfunctional Thoughts

5

"This is frustrating. I know it doesn't make sense but it seems so real."

As the student and counselor identify those thoughts, interpretive schemata, and core beliefs that are at the root of the student's dysfunctional feelings and actions, attention shifts to employing strategies to facilitate changes at all levels of cognition. Changing a student's dysfunctional beliefs is far from an easy task, even when the student is aware of the specific thoughts that are dysfunctional, and eager to reformulate these thoughts.

Even when our beliefs, our fundamental assumptions, and thoughts are clearly disruptive to our functioning, we are "wired" to retain them and expend energy to reshape and even distort reality (see Chapter 4) so that our experiences can be assimilated into these existing schemata. Thus, when helping a student reformulate these thoughts, the counselor will need to use a variety of strategies to provide the student with data that cannot be reshaped or reformulated to fit into the dysfunctional schema. If these data cannot be assimilated, the student will be forced to adjust the dysfunctional schema (accommodate) in order to accurately process these new data.

While the following chapter provides a number of specific strategies to be used by school counselors working from a cognitive orientation, the array of approaches a counselor could use is limited only by the counselor's imagination and the willingness of the student to participate. As long as the technique can "challenge" the student's dysfunctional thinking in a way that forces accommodation, the strategy will prove effective.

"JUST THINK NICE THOUGHTS"

The comedian, Al Franken, use to play a character on *Saturday Night Live* (NBC) called Stuart Smalley. Stuart was a person who promoted the value of self-affirmation. Stuart would look in the mirror and give himself daily affirmations, such as: "I deserve good things. I am entitled to my share of happiness. I refuse to beat myself up. I am an attractive person. I am fun to be with."

Often, those unfamiliar with the theory and research supporting the efficacy of a cognitive approach assume that it is fundamentally just a strategy promoting good feelings through the use of happy thoughts. This is not the case.

School counselors working with students experiencing real sadness, debilitating anxiety, or explosive anger understand that such daily affirmations do not address the real issues facing these students, nor do they help reformulate any of the student's core beliefs that may be exacerbating the real situation and resulting in additional upset. To some degree, there is value to having our students think positive and self-affirming thoughts, but real assistance is provided when those thoughts are embraced not just because they help the student feel good, but because they are accurate reflections of reality and facilitate the student's adjustment to the current challenges.

Counselors working with a cognitive orientation may direct students to engage in a variety of activities, including reading selective materials, or engaging in structured observations or mini-experiments all geared to producing the needed "ah, ha" and awareness of the impact of their dysfunctional thinking. This same directive approach would then be employed to facilitate the student's reformulation of thinking so that it is more reflective of the student's reality and facilitative of his or her adaptive feelings and actions. Table 5.1 illustrates a number of strategies that a counselor could use in confronting specific forms of cognitive distortion often presented by students.

In addition to directing the student to engage in such activities and experiences as a way of setting up the therapeutic cognitive dissonance, the school counselor employing a cognitive approach may model the process of "disputing" beliefs. The use of the counselor's sensitively timed confrontations invites the student to reconsider his or her perspective, in light of the "facts." Clearly, such an approach requires that the counselor and student have a good working alliance and the counselor has the skills to offer such therapeutic confrontations. Case Illustration 5.1 provides a view of one counselor's use of therapeutic challenge and directed teaching as a strategy to engage the student in the processes of debating, refuting, and reformulating dysfunctional beliefs.

Table 5.1   Intervention Targeting Specific Distortion

Cognitive Distortion	Underlying Fundamental Beliefs	Targets and Strategies for Intervention
Catastrophizing	Unless things are the way the student wants them to be, it is a disaster, and an unbearable situation.	Begin to identify the real—the most probable—worst-case scenario. What is the worst thing likely to happen? With this definition of outcome, ways of reducing negative outcome and/or developing a tolerance can be targeted.
Selective Abstracting	Only certain data are important to perceive and retain, and those things that do not fit the student's self-percept or view of the world are irrelevant and should be ignored or modified.	Have the student engage in mini-experiments and log all that happened, so that successes that have been discounted can be identified.
Dichotomous Thinking	Views of the world are very rigid and considered as either one extreme or another; the student sees everything as "black or white."	Have the student attempt to view situations from another's perspective as a way of introducing events to evaluate along a continuum.
Asserting Shoulds and Musts	An absolute sense of duty and right and wrong are embedded in the student's view that his or her way is the only way.	Invite the student to analyze the impact of replacing shoulds and musts with "wishes," "wants," and preferences. Also, invite the student to reframe beliefs that others "should" or "should not" to "if I made the rules for the world, then others would . . ."

Case Illustration 5.1   Nicole: Feeling Unlovable and Alone

Counselor:	So, Nicole, you did a really good job at keeping your thought log.
Nicole:	Thanks, but I'm not sure how it's going to help. It only proves I'm a loser!
Counselor:	Well, as we discussed last time, those feelings that you have of being very sad and worthless stem from your belief that you are not lovable and will be alone all of your life.
Nicole:	But that's true.
Counselor:	I know it feels true, but let me ask you a question. If we look at your beliefs as hypotheses rather than absolute facts, then it would be useful to "test" these against the evidence.
Nicole:	Yeah I did. Look at this (pointing to a log date). Brad called me and told me that he no longer wanted to go out and that he was going to date Mimi. See . . . loser!
Counselor:	I bet that was really unexpected and disappointing?
Nicole:	Disappointing . . . try devastating!
Counselor:	But I'm not sure I understand. It was devastating to hear that Brad, a guy you had dated for three weeks, no longer wanted to go out with you?
Nicole:	No, not just that. I mean, if Brad doesn't want me, I doubt anyone will!
Counselor:	Oh, so it wasn't the actual event that made you so sad?
Nicole:	Not really. Brad's a bit of a jerk and he smokes and I don't like that.
Counselor:	So, if we are focusing just on the actual event—you know, just like you wrote it here, in this first column (pointing to the paper), "Brad called and said he didn't want to go out anymore." If we just focused on that real life event, how would you feel?
Nicole:	Probably surprised, because I thought we were hitting it off. But you know what, as we are talking about it, I kind of feel relieved. I really wasn't enjoying going out with him, but I guess it was better than nothing?
Counselor:	Okay, so if you had that thought that it was a surprise, but actually it wasn't the relationship you really wanted, then you wouldn't have felt like you described here (pointing to her column describing the emotional consequences of the call). See, you wrote, "devastating, horrible, hated myself, scared of being alone for the rest of my life."
Nicole:	No . . . but that's how it felt.

Counselor: Well, Nicole, it felt that way because if you look here at your middle column, where you wrote down your self-talk, your beliefs, you know, how you were interpreting the situation, then I can see how it felt really horrible. Look (pointing to her description of her interpretation), you wrote down "I'm such a loser, no one will ever be interested in being with me. I'm going to be alone all my life; no one could love me." And truthfully, I guess that if this were true, that out of all the humans that existed you were the only one who no one—not your mom or grandma or best friend—would ever love, I guess that would be painful. But if the belief was just a hypothesis and not a statement of fact, could you find evidence to dispute it?

Nicole: Well, you already did. My mom does love me, actually my family really cares about me, and as you were talking I remembered all the friends I have and even poor Jeremy—he's a guy who has been dying to go out with me. So yeah, I can find a lot of facts that suggest that some people love me.

Counselor: Nicole, that's great. And, if you used your evidence to create a new belief, what do you think it would look like?

Nicole: Well, I guess I would have thought, "Damn, I didn't see this coming, but hey, I couldn't handle his smoking and to be honest I'm never real comfortable ending relationships. So okay, I'm probably not going out on a date this week . . . but there are other guys out there."

Counselor: That's super!

Nicole: Yeah, but that's now . . . not then! How am I ever going to learn?

Counselor: Well, I think there are two parts to that. First, you have to keep practicing hearing your interpretations, your beliefs, and learn to treat them like hypotheses that need to be tested before you buy them as truth. The second thing is to just think of this like learning a new language. You know, when you first learned the Spanish word for the color white you probably had to look it up, then write it down, and then read it. But the more you used it, you may have found that while you first thought "white," you may have quickly translated it into "blanco," and if you kept using the Spanish word and you saw a picture of something white, you would immediately go to the new language and think "blanco." Well, the same is true here. Maybe at first you will reformulate your thought— well, after the event. But eventually, with practice, you will reformulate as you are in the experience and eventually, you will begin to approach events with this new perspective.

(Continued)

(Continued)

Nicole: That makes sense. So, I guess it's practice, practice, practice...and (laughing) I guess that means I should keep my trusty journal next to me?

Counselor: Maybe not "next to you," but it's a great way to keep challenging your thinking. Also it doesn't hurt to maybe remind yourself—maybe by writing a little note or post-it—that your thoughts are "hypotheses" about you and your world, and should be tested for supportive evidence.

Nicole: Got it...hypotheses!

LOOKING FOR THE EVIDENCE

Challenging students' beliefs is not an easy process, since they have developed a lot of personal evidence to convince them that these beliefs make sense. The school counselor needs to help students appreciate the difficulty in changing their core beliefs. Students need to be encouraged to see these core beliefs as "hypotheses" and not automatic facts. If the counselor can help a student "see" these beliefs as working hypotheses, the student can then be supported in the process of testing those beliefs against alternative views of that same reality. The goal is to help the student develop more reflective thoughts of the reality being experienced—be it positive, negative, or neutral—and thus provide the basis for a more adaptive and functional response.

One technique to facilitate this process is to have the student employ the seven-column thought log (see Figure 5.1).

The process invites the student to suspend judgment and conviction that his or her thoughts are "factual," rather than subjective interpretations about experiences and events in his or her life—interpretations that may be supported by the evidence, but may just as likely be distortions and thus not supported by reality. The student will be invited to embrace the personal beliefs as "hypotheses" rather than "facts" and as hypotheses need to be tested for accuracy. With this as the framework, the student will be invited to gather data needed to "test" these thoughts. In Case Illustration 5.2, the brief exchange between Tamara, a third-grade student, and her counselor illustrates how this process may appear.

Figure 5.1   The Seven-Column Method

Seven-Column Thought Log (Prompts)						
Event or Situation Include who, what, when, and where.	*Feelings* Describe how you were feeling and rate the feeling on a scale of 0–100%.	*Thoughts/Beliefs/ Meaning Making* What was going through your mind—the self-talk occurring at the time of your emotional arousal?	*What evidence supports your hypothesis about what this event "meant"?*	*What evidence do you have that fails to support your thought and your interpretation?*	*An Alternative View* Write an alternative viewpoint that seems to find greater support by the data. Also, rate the degree to which you believe that thought.	*Reevaluation of Mood* After reading your alternative view, reevaluate your current state in relationship to the mood you describe in column 2.

Seven-Column Thought Log (Sample Response)						
Event or Situation Well, I just finished taking the midterm. I really studied for it and yet it was really hard. I was one of the last people to finish the test.	*Feelings* I was almost sick to my stomach, really worried, and bummed out (80%).	*Thoughts/Beliefs/ Meaning Making* Damn, I really blew that. My grade is going to be in the toilet and there is no way I'll get honors this term. This is horrible; these are the grades that go to the colleges.	*What evidence supports your hypothesis?* Well, the test was hard and I left two of the fifty multiple choice unanswered, and I only wrote one page on the fourth and final essay.	*What evidence do you have that fails to support your thought and your interpretation?* Two of the four essays were things I thought he would ask and I had really prepared those. Also, the first sheet of multiple choice was easy. And, when we were talking about it at lunch, I seemed to have a lot of the same answers as Angie and she always gets 100s.	*An Alternative View* That test was really hard. I studied for it and I know I nailed two of the four essays. Most of my multiple-choice answers were the same as Angie's and she usually gets 100s, but I am concerned about the final two essays and what that could do to my grade.	*Reevaluation of Mood* I feel nervous (40%), and want to see how I did but I am also wondering if I do poorly if I could do extra-credit work to boost my final grade.

73

Case Illustration 5.2   Tamara: Approaching Thoughts as Hypotheses

Counselor:	Tamara, have you ever noticed the way you, or maybe your parents, eat soup?
Tamara:	Huh?
Counselor:	Yeah, sorry, that was a pretty silly question. What I meant was, do you know what people do when they get something like soup, or pizza, or anything from the oven that they think may be very hot? Do you know how they look as they start to eat it?
Tamara:	Oh you mean, like if it is hot, they blow on it?
Counselor:	Yeah. But what else do they do?
Tamara:	I don't know. Maybe they stick their tongue out like this (demonstrating) to feel how hot it is.
Counselor:	Great observations. I wonder why they do that? It does look funny.
Tamara:	Yeah (sticking out her tongue, and giggling).
Counselor:	Why do you think they do that?
Tamara:	To see if it is hot.
Counselor:	It's like, they make a prediction, "Hmm, the pizza looks hot," and therefore, before they take a big bite, they check out their prediction. That's a good thing. If they are correct and the pizza is hot, they can burn their mouths.
Tamara:	I did that.
Counselor:	Ouch! But their prediction could be wrong. You know, if the pizza is just right, then what?
Tamara:	I dig in!
Counselor:	I bet you do. So, I would like you and I to start to look at the "predictions" you make when you are in class. You know, like the thoughts we wrote down yesterday about the kids making fun of you if you make a mistake? Well, that's a prediction and just like the one regarding the pizza, it could be correct or it may be incorrect . . . so we need to test it (sticking tongue out, as if testing the pizza), to see if it is true or false.

Once the student understands and accepts the approach of reviewing thoughts as "predictions" or "hypotheses" and not immediate facts, he or she will be guided through the process of identifying evidence that would support the belief and list this support in the fourth column. Then returning to the initial thought, the student will be invited to look for evidence that fails to support, or is contrary to, the original thought. These data would be listed in the next column. The data to include in the log will be acquired either by the student's own self-reflections or through the sensitive questioning of the school counselor in session with the student. Often, the counselor-directed approach may be needed when working with younger students.

The idea is not to suggest that the original thought contained no elements of truth; rather, the purpose is to facilitate the student's processing of all the data—both confirming and disconfirming—and develop an alternative thought that incorporates all of these data (see Case Illustration 5.3)

| Case Illustration 5.3 | Carlos: Checking Thinking Against the Evidence |

Counselor:	Carlos, you really did a great job with collecting information in the thought log. What I want to do today is show you how we sometimes immediately assume what we are thinking about an event is absolute truth, but in fact, our thoughts are simply our best guess about things and sometimes we can be correct, and sometimes our guess may be way off base.
Carlos:	Yeah, I know what you mean. I thought I blew the history midterm, and when I got it back I was surprised I got a B.
Counselor:	Great example. The sad point is that if we really believe that our prediction of "blowing it" is true, we could end up needlessly worrying about something that really is not a bad event.
Carlos:	Tell me about it. I was all bummed out.
Counselor:	But how do you feel now?
Carlos:	Super!
Counselor:	And you feel super now, because?
Carlos:	'Cause I got a B!
Counselor:	So, this new information is used to change your thoughts and your feelings. But, I wonder if there was any information that you had yesterday, which if you really had considered, may have reduced the degree to which you were feeling bummed out?
Carlos:	I'm not sure what you mean.
Counselor:	Well, let's see if we can figure this out. See this form (pointing to the seven-column format)?
Counselor:	So, if I understand what you are saying, you had your midterm yesterday, and you really prepared for it. But, it was really difficult and you were one of the last ones to finish. Is that correct?

(Continued)

(Continued)

Carlos: Yeah, it was killer.

Counselor: Well, how about writing down that description in the first column (see Figure 5.1). And, maybe you could list how you felt after the test, and maybe even your thoughts, just like you did before in the thought log. Great. Now, this is the part I wanted to show you. I know you were almost absolutely sure you blew it and you were screwing up your college chances, but for now, let's see those thoughts as predictions, hypotheses, and let's see if we can find any evidence that may have supported them.

Carlos: Like the fact that I left some multiple choice questions unanswered and I was barely able to complete the essays.

Counselor: Okay, let's write the evidence down, but remember just list the facts . . . great. Now, if we continue with our fact finding, were there any facts that do not seem to support the notion that you blew it, or that you screwed up your chances for getting into a good school?

Carlos: You mean now? I got a B.

Counselor: No, I mean if we could review what actually happened during the test and list these events as supporting or not supporting your original hypothesis about failing, what would be placed in this column (pointing to fifth column) that would fail to support your hypothesis?

Carlos: Got it. Things like (writing in fifth column), I really got the first two essays and most of the multiple choice on the first page and, oh yeah, Angie and I agreed on most answers and she always gets 100s.

Counselor: Super. Now, could you rewrite your thought so that it would accurately reflect all of this information, these facts, and place that in column 6? You really are good at this. Now, if you believed that thought—which seems more supported by all of the data present—how do you think you may feel and act? Write that down in column 6.

When working with our students and helping them search for evidence that fails to support their initial hypotheses, it helps to have them consider the following questions:

a. If I were in another person's shoes, would I see it the same way?

b. If my friend or loved one were in this situation, believing what I am believing, what would I say to him or her?

c. If I look back on this event in three months, a year, or five years, will I see it differently?

It also needs to be highlighted that the goal of this exercise is not to simply help with this one event. It is not the content of what is written that holds the ultimate value, but rather the process of writing and eventually thinking in this manner. It is hoped with practice, the student who employs the seven-column method will learn to view all of the future evaluative thoughts as hypotheses rather than facts, and with that perspective, immediately search for evidence supporting each hypothesis or an alternative. If we return to an earlier illustration of the thinking-feeling connection, we can see where a child lying in bed hears a noise and concludes that there is a monster in the room. Given this "fact," this "reality," the child feels and acts terrified. However, that same child, who hears a noise and asks, "What is that?" starts to generate multiple possibilities, multiple hypotheses, such as it is a monster, my mother, a floor board, a branch at the window, etc. The child then becomes aroused and curious and will immediately be moved to gather data in order to find support for the one best hypothesis. This is the *process* that the school counselor is attempting to teach his or her student.

MINI-EXPERIMENTS

When students are unable to gather accurate thought logs, testing their thinking is possible by using mini-experiments. If the counselor can help the student see that the core beliefs are neither correct nor incorrect but are predictions—hypotheses that may or may not be valid in any one situation—then perhaps the student will engage as "researcher," in testing his or her core beliefs. In this situation, the student is asked to engage in mini-experiments designed specifically to test core beliefs. During this process, the student, with the counselor's support, identifies specific actions that can be taken to, in his or her mind, provide support for the core belief. The student is asked to identify the core belief being tested as well as the prediction of the outcome of this experiment. With these points identified, the student is then invited to test the hypothesis by engaging in the activity and recording the actual outcome. These data are then reviewed and discussed in session as illustrated by the following interaction between Lenny, a fourth-grade student, and his counselor.

Counselor: Okay (smiling), are you ready for the big experiment?

Lenny: I guess.

Counselor: Well, if we got it right, it seems that you are afraid to ask the guys if you can join in playing basketball at recess because you "know" they don't like you, and won't let you play. Is that correct?

Lenny: Yeah, they don't like me. No one in this school does.

Counselor: Well, remember yesterday when we were talking? We decided that your thinking that "no one likes you" may or may not be an actual fact. And the best way to figure that out is to maybe test it? So, what have you decided you could do to test that thought to see if it is an accurate or inaccurate prediction?

Lenny: Well, I brought my new basketball to school today and I thought I would just go out at lunch and shoot some baskets on the other court, the one those guys aren't using.

Counselor: That's neat. What do you think will happen?

Lenny: Somebody is going to say something, something wise, like "look at the loser."

Counselor: Okay. Let's write some things down.

Experiment	Belief	Prediction	What Happened
Take basketball and shoot baskets.	No one likes me.	Someone will call me a loser.	

Counselor: Now, your job is to go out today and give it a try, but remember you're a "researcher," so write down everything that happens. I will see you later and we can talk about it. Okay?

The counselor would meet with Lenny following the mini-experiment in order to review and discuss the experience. The focus of the discussion would be on identifying those data that supported the initial prediction as well as data that failed to support that belief and rather supported an alternative viewpoint. With the counselor's support, the student would then be helped to reformulate the belief so that it more accurately reflected all of the data collected.

Counselor: Lenny, I'm so proud of you. You did a great job! So tell me, what happened?

Lenny: I went out and I was there before everyone came out to play, and see I told you (pointing to the "What Happened" column), Jeremiah hollered, "Hey loser, nice ball."

Counselor: Hmm, so you predicted someone would call you a loser. But I'm wondering, is that all that happened? I also wonder if the fact that this one student, Jeremiah, said something is evidence that "no one" likes you.

Lenny: I don't know.

Counselor: Well, what else happened?

Lenny: They started to form teams and they were one short so Jamal asked if I wanted to play, and then Jeremiah said, "And bring your new ball, loser!"

Counselor: Wow. So you played?

Lenny: Yeah.

Counselor: What does the fact that Jamal invited you to play and the others kids, even Jeremiah, let you play, mean? How does that fit in with your belief that "no one" likes you?

Lenny: I don't know. Maybe these guys were just being nice this time because they needed someone and I had a new ball.

Counselor: Well, you know, that might be true, but remember that is just a prediction, a hypothesis. What else may explain what happened?

Lenny: Well, maybe some of the guys like me?

Counselor: Okay, so an alternative way of looking at it is that some of the guys like you and maybe some guys don't care for you? But this too is a prediction that we should test? What kind of things could we look for that would test these ideas—either that some like you and some may not, or they were only playing because they needed you, or even some other possible way of looking at the situation?

Lenny: I guess if they were nice to me at lunch or if they let me play tomorrow even if I didn't bring my ball.

Counselor: Fantastic! Great idea. So I will check in with you tomorrow and see what happened.

As the counselor continues to work with Lenny, he would try to assist Lenny in reframing his core belief from "No one likes me" to something like, "There are some people who may not be friendly to me but others who will." Also, the counselor would assist Lenny in employing this "hypotheses-testing" approach to all of his beliefs.

When engaging students in these mini-experiments, the school counselor should select small situations where outcomes, even in the worst-case scenario, are both predictable and tolerable. The counselor working with Lenny would first want to feel confident that the guys playing in the yard really didn't dislike Lenny and that the probability of them making fun of him, calling him a loser, and totally rejecting him was low. But even when things don't go as hoped, the data collected can still be used to test the absolute nature of the original prediction. This will provide the counselor with an opportunity to help the student generate alternative interpretations and embrace a hypotheses-testing approach to his or her thinking. Consider the following case illustration of Ellie, a third-grade student who simply "knows" no one likes her and who "knows" that everyone will be mean to her.

Case Illustration 5.4	Ellie: No One Likes Me

Counselor:	So Ellie, if someone doesn't like another person, would they do favors for that person?
Ellie:	You mean like give them things or do something for them?
Counselor:	Yep, that's the kind of thing I mean by doing favors.
Ellie:	I don't think so.
Counselor:	Okay, and therefore, when you say things like nobody in class likes you, I guess that means no one in class would do you a favor?
Ellie:	No way.
Counselor:	So for example, Jason or Tanya or Alexandra—they wouldn't lend you a pencil if you asked to borrow one? Or they wouldn't tell you what was due for homework or anything like that?
Ellie:	They don't like me, no one does (starting to get upset).
Counselor:	I understand. But I'm wondering if you would be willing to do a little "experiment" for me?
Ellie:	I guess.
Counselor:	Great. I know you were doing reading activities in class when you came down. How about if you pick out one person in the class and when you go back, ask him or her what page you are on. Would you do that?
Ellie:	I guess I could ask Tanya. She sits at my table, but why?
Counselor:	Well, you are making a prediction that no one likes you, and then you and I agreed that when people dislike other people they probably wouldn't do them favors. So, if you ask Tanya the page the class is on, we may be able to see if she gives you that information or not?

Ellie:	She won't and I feel stupid?
Counselor:	Is it stupid to ask someone for information?
Ellie:	No, but...
Counselor:	If Tanya doesn't tell you, what else could you do?
Ellie:	I could ask Mrs. Hackney.
Counselor:	Great. So, you could ask Tanya and if she doesn't tell you, you could simply ask your teacher and then start reading like the other students. No big deal, right?
Ellie:	I guess.
Counselor:	So, how about if you try our little experiment and I will see you at the end of school today to see how it went?

It is possible that, when doing these mini-experiments, the student may actually experience outcomes pointing to a deficit in some area of skill or knowledge. For example, there is a chance that Ellie's request for help from Tanya may go unheeded. Tanya may not tell Ellie which page the class is reviewing. But even in this situation, the counselor could help Ellie develop multiple hypotheses about why Tanya failed to give her the information. For example, perhaps Tanya didn't respond because she: (1) doesn't like Ellie, (2) didn't know the answer, or (3) didn't hear or understand the request (among other such possibilities). Generating and discussing the possibility of these other propositions would help Ellie employ the process of generating multiple interpretations of an event and look for that interpretation which reflects all of the data.

In processing the actual outcomes of the experiment, the counselor will want to identify areas of strength as well as areas where skill or knowledge development would be beneficial. For example, in reviewing the data, the counselor and Ellie determine that the problem is that Tanya simply did not hear the request because Ellie tends to speak in a very low tone. The counselor would thus not only help Ellie confront her faulty interpretation about the situation, but may assist her to develop more direct and assertive behavior. This is also the situation illustrated in the case of the counselor working with Roberto.

Case Illustration 5.5 Roberto: I'll Die

Counselor:	Well? How was the dance?
Roberto:	It was okay, I guess.
Counselor:	Yeah, but how about our mini-experiment? Did you ask Maria to dance?
Roberto:	Yeah. Not so good though.
Counselor:	Not so good?
Roberto:	Well, I waited until almost the last song. I was nervous as all get out. But I kept saying to myself, "I'm not going to die. This isn't the end of the world."
Counselor:	Super.
Roberto:	Well yeah, but anyway . . . I walk over and I feel like everybody is looking at me as I am walking across to floor to where she's standing. I get there and I am so nervous my knees are shaking and my voice is cracking and I say, "Hey, want to dance?"
Counselor:	That's great, you actually asked her to dance?
Roberto:	Yeah (smiling). Well she looks at me, and then says, "Me?" and I almost panic and run away. But, then I just said, "Yeah, want to dance?"
Counselor:	I'm proud of you hanging in there.
Roberto:	She says, "No, thanks" and I go, "Okay" and start to walk back where my friends are, feeling like whew that was painful.
Counselor:	It was painful because?
Roberto:	Well, I was thinking I made a complete jerk out of myself.
Counselor:	Really? What are you using as evidence for that?
Roberto:	Well, she said "no thanks."
Counselor:	So, everyone who asks someone to have or do something, and in response get a no thanks, they're all . . . jerks?
Roberto:	No, but it sure felt like it.
Counselor:	Roberto, what other things could you identify that would suggest you were not, as you say, a jerk, but actually maybe even pretty cool or gutsy?
Roberto:	Well, I was the only one of my friends who did that, even though a couple of the guys kept talking about asking her to dance. They just talked and never did ask her.

Counselor:	Great. Anything else?
Roberto:	Well, I didn't die (laughing).
Counselor:	You certainly didn't!
Roberto:	But boy, was I a mess.
Counselor:	Well, I'm wondering, I know she wasn't interested in dancing, but maybe there would be a better approach to asking a girl to dance. I mean, if you approach her with, you know, knees knocking, voice cracking, and give her a quick invite . . . I wonder if your approach was a little less than smooth and that may be one of the reasons she said "no thanks"?
Roberto:	Less than smooth . . . man, it was pathetic!
Counselor:	Well, you've come to the right spot. I'm the master of smooth (smiling). So, if you would be willing to try an experiment again, maybe we could first clean up your approach and see what happens.
Roberto:	Sure, the doctor of smooth is in the house (laughing).

However, the real value of the experiment is that it provides data that contradicted Roberto's absolute and catastrophic thinking that he "would die" or at least be totally and unbearably humiliated if his invitation to dance was rejected. Reframing the situations as less catastrophic would automatically reduce Roberto's anxiety and with it, most likely reduce his anxious style and demeanor. This is the real benefit to mini-experiments as it allows the counselor the opportunity to teach the student to use the data to challenge his or her tendency to embrace the hypotheses as irrefutable facts.

ACTING "AS IF"

Another approach to facilitate a student's understanding of the impact of changing his or her thoughts on resultant feelings and actions is to encourage the student to act "as if." This is often a valuable technique to employ once an alternative view of the situation has been articulated. Acting as if invites the student to "try on" a new way of thinking, and with it, experience outcomes that support the "validity" of this new, alternative perspective on self, and/or the world. Consider the following exchange between Melissa and her counselor in Case Illustration 5.6.

Case Illustration 5.6	Melissa: Acting "As If"

Counselor:	Melissa, so you tell me you can stand on stage in front of an auditorium full of people, and sing your song or say your lines, but you feel like you will throw up when you have to do a presentation in class?
Melissa:	It's different. On stage I'm playing a role. You know, I'm someone else.
Counselor:	I think I get it. So, when you step into a role and act like that character, it is easier for you to perform in front of people without feeling like you are going to panic?
Melissa:	Yeah, exactly.
Counselor:	Hmm, so if you had a script and you were playing the role of "confident" and "competent" student, who is well-liked and very capable of giving a class presentation—if you had that as a role in a play—you think you could give a presentation?
Melissa:	Yeah (smiling), I guess.
Counselor:	What do you think (smiling)? Want the role? Why not try a mini-experiment? When you have to get up in class and do your presentation, why not try to step into that role, you know, act as if you are the confident, competent, well-liked student written into the script. Would you be willing to try that?
Melissa:	I could try. In fact, I have an oral report due on Friday.
Counselor:	Well, give it a try and then we can sit down and discuss how it went?

The counselor working with Melissa is not attempting to encourage her to pretend she is someone that she isn't. Rather, the data shows that Melissa *is* competent and well-liked; what she *is not* is confident, and acting "as if" may help her to not only be successful but provide the evidence she needs to truly believe that she is competent. This belief will add to her self-confidence, reduce her anxiety, and facilitate her ability to provide class presentations.

FROM A COUNSELING TECHNIQUE TO A LIFE APPROACH

While the student may come to the counselor with a specific issue or upsetting situation that serves as the initial target for the counseling, and even though the strategies presented here will help the student reframe this situation, the positive impact need not stop there. As the counselor explained to Nicole (see Case Illustration 5.1), the more the student employs the process of cognitive disputing and learns to replace dysfunctional beliefs with more functional thinking, the more "automatic" this way of thinking will become. With use and practice, the techniques presented in the counseling session will be assimilated as the student's approach to life.

In the early sessions, the student may complain that writing things down, after the fact, seems silly. It is not unusual for students to report that using the seven-column approach in reference to a particular upsetting situation feels phony or artificial. To some degree it is. This process is not one that they are familiar with, nor initially comfortable. A parallel to this might be the experience a student has had learning a foreign language. Initially when learning a new language, the student may first have to stop, and actually look up the translation for a particular item. With more practice, he or she will be able to pause and mentally translate the item from English into the new language. As the student continues to practice, this new language can become like his or her native tongue. Items can be spontaneously interpreted through the lens of that new language, while the student is unaware that the translations occur while converting the experience from old language to new, and the student may even dream in this new language. The same is true for rational thinking. With practice, what may at first have felt like an artificial technique or counseling strategy, can become the process of choice—a process that colors the student's approach to life events and results in more adaptable, and functional, feelings and actions.

CONSIDERATIONS FOR YOUNGER STUDENTS

While the unique focus of cognitive counseling is the identification, confrontation, and reformulation of a student's dysfunctional thinking, as with any model of counseling, the school counselor employing a cognitive orientation needs to engage the student in a warm, empathetic relationship. With empathy, the school counselor will adjust strategies in order to make them more developmentally appropriate.

The counselor working with older students can teach the student to change his or her thinking by employing Socratic questioning, thought logs/journals, and mini-experiments. However, when working with younger students (i.e., PreK–Grade 2), the use of expressive materials and techniques along with structured worksheets, concrete illustrations, and parable-type stories may prove more effective. Similarly, when attempting to "debate" the thinking of younger students, the school counselor with cognitive orientation may want to employ less direct methods of confrontation.

Table 5.2 provides a sampling of structured materials that are useful when working with our younger students. As noted earlier, those working with younger students may want to review the additional resources at the end of this chapter.

Table 5.2   Structured Materials for Younger Students

Area	Resource
Anxiety	*Ready, Set, Relax: A Research-Based Program of Relaxation, Learning and Self-Esteem for Children* (1997) by Jeffrey Allen and Roger Klein
Social Skills	*Raise Your Child's Social IQ: Stepping Stones to People Skills for Kids* (2000) by Cathi Cohen
Depression, Sadness, and Low Self-Esteem	*The Optimistic Child: Proven Program to Safeguard Children from Depression & Build Lifelong Resilience* (1996) by Martin Seligman
Self-Esteem and Rational Problem Solving	*Raising Resilient Children: Fostering Strength, Hope, and Optimism in Your Child* (2002) by Robert Brooks and Sam Goldstein
Anxiety	*Worried No More: Help and Hope for Anxious Children* (2005) by Aureen Wagner
OCD	*Up and Down the Worry Hill: A Children's Book about Obsessive-Compulsive Disorder and Its Treatment* (2004) by Aureen Wagner
Anger	*When Sophie Gets Angry—Really, Really Angry . . .* (2004) by Molly Bang
Self-Esteem and Valuing Individual Uniqueness	*Odd Velvet* (1998) by Mary Whitcomb and Tara Calahan-King
Self-Esteem and Valuing Individual Uniqueness	*The Tenth Good Thing About Barney* (1987) by Judith Viorstand Erik Blegavd
Coping With Bullying	*Enemy Pie* (2000) by Derek Munson and Tara Calahan-King

WHAT'S NEXT?

Now that the theory and techniques have been described, we will move on to see their application. However, unlike the cases found within this section, the cases presented in Part III provide us with a glimpse of the counselor's thinking. We will see how a counselor using a cognitive framework will process student data both in session and between sessions to guide decisions and treatment planning.

SUMMARY

Reformulating Dysfunctional Thinking

- When helping a student reformulate these thoughts, the counselor will need to use a variety of strategies to provide the student with data that cannot be reshaped or reformulated to fit into the dysfunctional schema. If these data cannot be assimilated, the student will be forced to adjust the dysfunctional schema (accommodate) in order to accurately process these new data.
- If the counselor can help the student "see" his or her beliefs as working hypotheses, the counselor can support the student in the process of testing those beliefs against alternative views of that same reality. The goal is to help the student develop thoughts that are more reflective of the reality being experienced—be it positive, negative, or neutral and thus provide the basis for a more adaptive and functional response.
- When working with our students and helping them search for evidence that fails to support their initial hypothesis, it helps to have them consider the following questions:
  - a. If I were in another person's shoes, would I see it the same way?
  - b. If my friend or loved one were in this situation, believing what I am believing, what would I say to him or her?
  - c. If I look back on this event in three months, a year, or five years, will I see it differently?

Mini-Experiments

- If the student embraces the core beliefs as neither correct nor incorrect but as predictions, hypotheses that may or may not be

(Continued)

(Continued)

valid in any one situation, then perhaps the student will engage as "researcher," conducting mini-experiments for testing of these core beliefs.

Acting "As If"

- Another approach to facilitating a student's understanding of the impact of changing his or her thoughts on resultant feelings and actions is to encourage the student to act "as if."
- Acting as if invites the student to "try on" a new way of thinking, and with it, experience outcomes that support the "validity" of this new, alternative perspective on self, and/or the world.

Working With Various Age Groups

- The counselor working with older students can teach the student to change his or her thinking by employing Socratic questioning, thought logs/journals, and mini-experiments.
- When working with younger students (i.e., PreK–Grade 2), the use of expressive materials and techniques along with structured worksheets, concrete illustrations, and parable-type stories may prove more effective.
- When attempting to "debate" the thinking of younger students, the school counselor with cognitive orientation may want to employ less direct methods of confrontation.

ADDITIONAL RESOURCES FOR WORKING WITH YOUNGER STUDENTS

Albert Ellis Institute (2009). *The Albert Ellis Institute: Short term therapy, long term results*. Retrieved March 5, 2009 from http://www.rebt.org/.

Berg, B. (1990). *The depression management game*. Dayton, OH: Cognitive Counseling Resources.

Ellis, A., Bernard, M. E. (2006). *Rational emotive behavioral approaches to childhood disorders: Theory, practice and research*. Boston: Birkhauser.

Freeman, A., Pretzer, J., Fleming, B., & Simon, K. (2004). *Clinical applications of cognitive therapy* (2nd ed.). New York: Kluwer Academic/Plenum Publications.

Friedberg, R. D. (1996). Cognitive-behavioral games and workbooks: Tips for school counselors. *Elementary School Guidance & Counseling, 31* (1), 11–21.

Greensberger, D., & Padesky, C. A. (1995). *Mind over mood*. New York: Guildford.

Kendall, P. C. (1988). *The stop and think workbook*. Philadelphia: Temple University.

Kendall, P. C. (1990). *Coping cat workbook.* Philadelphia: Temple University.

Piper, W. (1976). *The little engine that could: The complete original edition.* New York: Platt and Munk.

Reinecke, M. A., Dattilio, F. M., Freeman, A., Lopez, C., & Parra, G. (2003). *Cognitive therapy with children and adolescents: A casebook for clinical practice* (2nd ed.). New York: Guildford.

Stallard, P. (2003). *Think good—feel good: A cognitive behaviour therapy workbook for children and young people.* New York: Wiley & Sons.

Vernon, A. (1989). *Thinking, feeling, behaving: An emotional education curriculum for adolescents/grades 7–12.* Champaign, IL: Research Press.

Vernon, A. (2002). *What works when with children and adolescents: A handbook of individual counseling techniques.* Champaign, IL: Research Press.

Vernon, A. (2005). *Thinking, feeling, behaving: An emotional education curriculum for children/grades 1–6.* Champaign, IL: Research Press.

Vernon, A., & Al-Mabuk, R. (1995). *What growing up is all about.* Champaign, IL: Research Press.

Woods, P. J. (1996). Rational emotive behavior therapy has a humanistic orientation—definitely. *The Journal of Humanistic Education and Development,* 35, 89–92.

Wright, J., Basco, M. R., & Thase, M. (2005). *Learning cognitive-behavior therapy: An illustrated guide.* Arlington, VA: American Psychiatric Publishing.

Part III

From the Eyes of the Cognitive-Oriented Expert

The previous chapters introduced the principles, constructs, and strategies of a cognitive-oriented approach to school counseling. However, the primary purpose of this book is to assist counselors in the process of "thinking" like a cognitively oriented counselor, and not merely understanding principles and concepts. But what does "thinking" like an expert entail?

A review of the literature identifying differences between "expert" and "novice" professionals points to the fact that those with expertise encode, organize, and use client information in ways to facilitate reasoning and problem solving much differently than those new to the profession. Rather than organizing student data into categories that are based on superficial, irrelevant cues that may not be pertinent to generating a problem solution, experts employ organizational cognitive structures, or schemas, to help them quickly make sense of the information that a student is presenting (Chi, Feltovich, & Glaser, 1981). Student data are stored in problem-relevant categories that are connected by underlying conceptual principles relevant to the problem solution.

In addition to employing more effective organizational cognitive structures to discern the relevant from the irrelevant, and to store these data efficiently, experts employ procedural knowledge to guide their interactions with students while in session. The effective counselor actively reflects on the information provided by the student and uses those data to guide his or her own reactions and interventions. The effective, "expert," school counselor approaches counseling by organizing the material presented by the student into "If [condition phase], then [action phase]" statements. The expert counselor knows that, "If the student presents with this, then I'll do that."

Developing the ability to employ a cognitive-orienting framework guides this "If . . . , then" procedural thinking, in order to know what to do and when to do it, and leads to an increase in the school counselor's effectiveness. Developing procedural thinking requires that we move beyond simply understanding, and storing concepts and constructs, and begin to employ these concepts in practice. The final two chapters of this book (Chapter 6 and 7) are designed to support the development of this procedural knowledge using a cognitive-orienting framework to guide you and your reflective practice.

Chapter 6 provides an in-depth look at two school counselors in action as they address student concerns using a cognitive-orienting framework. Each case provides a look into the methods and strategies employed by a counselor with a cognitive focus. However, more than an illustration of the application of cognitive strategies, each case also provides some insight into the counselor's procedural thinking—that is, at any one moment, what guides the selection and use of these "strategies." This insight into the counselor's thought processes while engaging with the student will show you how to employ a cognitive orientation to both process the data presented by these students and anticipate the needed counselor's responses. It is in developing that anticipation that you will have employed procedural knowledge from a cognitive orientation, thus "thinking" like the expert!

In Chapter 7, you are invited to become an active participant in the processes of reflective practice. As was the situation with the case material found in Chapter 6, student data and verbatim exchanges are provided, but in Chapter 7 there will be a number of points in the encounter where you will be invited to stop and reflect on the data presented, and then anticipate the direction to be taken. You will then have the opportunity to see the choices made by the counselor in this situation as well as that counselor's "thinking" that guided the decision and direction. It is hoped that this vicarious engagement with the case materials, along with the ability to contrast your thinking with that of the scripted counselor, will help you move beyond simply knowing and understanding, to now owning and doing school counseling from a cognitive orientation.

School Counselors Reflecting "in" and "on" Practice **6**

The current chapter invites you to begin using the process of cognitive orientation as the filter through which to interpret student data and to begin to devise intervention strategies. In this chapter, two cases will be presented, each illustrating a school counselor's use of a cognitive-orienting model to guide reflective practice. As noted in the introduction to Part III, it is suggested that as you review each of the cases and observe the interaction between the student and counselor, you attempt to use your understanding of a cognitive-orienting model to anticipate the counselors thinking and subsequent action.

In the first case, the school counselor illustrates her reflections starting with her review of the initial referral. Even with these preliminary data, this counselor begins to generate an initial hypothesis about what may be going on, and uses these as the springboard for her case conceptualization and treatment planning. Once engaged with the student, the counselor demonstrates her ability to be flexible and adjust to the specific needs of the student, and to the data being presented at any one moment in that encounter. It is her reflections during practice that allow her to adjust her interventions in process to help this student grasp the connection of thought to feelings.

The second case highlights the various strategies employed by a counselor as he attempts to help the student identify cognitive errors and dysfunctional thoughts, and then challenge those thoughts. As you read the illustration, you will become aware of the power of our natural resistance to cognitive change. However, you will also see how the effective use of Socratic questioning creates a condition of cognitive tension, or dissonance, to facilitate the student's ability to reformulate his cognitive distortions into more adaptable ways of thinking.

CASE 1: PRISCILLA

Starting with the initial intake, the effective school counselor allows his or her counseling decisions to be guided by a process of gathering data, reflecting on that data, and then, through the use of an operative model, drawing conclusions to direct his or her actions. For the counselor operating from a cognitive-orienting framework, a number of markers are set out to guide this reflection and the resulting practice decisions (see Figure 6.1). In this first case, the case of Priscilla, we will "see" the counselor's reflection and practice decisions as she moves from the initial referral through to engaging the student in identifying her personal thought-feeling connections.

Figure 6.1   Guiding Reflection and Practice Decisions

Establish Relationship

(Establish a working alliance with the student.)

Discern Real From Perceived Issues

(Identify and discern the real issues confronting the student from his or her interpretation of these events.)

Thought-Feeling Connection

(Help the student understand and embrace the thought-feeling connection.)

Beliefs and Assumptions

(Drill down to personal beliefs and operative assumptions.)

Cognitive Distortions

(Review concept and personal experience with cognitive distortions.)

Confront and Reform

(Develop/implement intervention strategies to confront and reformulate dysfunctional beliefs and cognitive distortions.)

Monitor and Adjust

Plan for Maintenance and Relapse Prevention

Initial Referral

Priscilla is a second-grade student referred to the school counselor, Mrs. O'Malley, by her teacher, Ms. Elkin, who is concerned that Priscilla is having difficulty completing tasks and appears to get very upset and anxious if she does not get a 100 on each assignment. In the referral, the teacher states:

> I am a bit concerned about Priscilla's apparent anxiety about her grades and performance in class. I've had a number of occasions where I would literally have to go down to Priscilla's desk and tell her it was time to stop working on a particular assignment and that she needed to hand it in. She almost always protested, asking for more time to check her work.

> However, yesterday she had a total meltdown in class—crying and pleading that I give her more time to check her answers on a test. She was so out of control—crying and shaking—that I had to take her to the nurse's office. I'm really concerned about her. She seems to worry too much about her grades and performance. She is a gifted child but seems to me somewhat of a perfectionist.

Reflections Prior to Meeting

As Mrs. O'Malley reads the referral, she immediately begins to "hypothesize" about the possible nature and source of this apparent overreaction. It appears that, for Priscilla, the possibility of producing less than "perfect" work is not simply unacceptable, but truly intolerable and catastrophic.

Having previously spoken to Priscilla's mom and dad, Mrs. O'Malley is sure that the presence of real negative physical or emotional threats or consequences in the event that Priscilla performs poorly is not a real possibility. As such, she hypothesizes that Priscilla's reactions are the result of her own misinterpretation of the necessity of "being perfect."

Armed with this operating hypothesis, Mrs. O'Malley hopes to engage Priscilla in counseling with a cognitive orientation. As she prepares to meet with Priscilla, Mrs. O'Malley reflects on the need to employ all her skills to establish a warm, working relationship with Priscilla. Further, she hopes that she will be able to help Priscilla begin to understand the difference between the facts of being less than perfect, and her belief in what that would mean. The one thing that Mrs. O'Malley knows for certain is that she wants to be sure that Priscilla does not view coming to the counselor's office as a sign of her being a failure.

Session 1: Establishing a Working Alliance

Mrs. O: Good morning, Priscilla. Thanks for coming down to talk with me.

Priscilla: You're welcome.

Mrs. O: As you probably know, I'm Mrs. O'Malley, and I am the school counselor.

(Continued)

(Continued)

Priscilla: I knew that.

Mrs. O: You did? That's great. What else do you know about what I do at the school?

Priscilla: You talk to the students.

Mrs. O: That's correct. I talk with the students and sometimes help them with some things that may be troubling them.

Priscilla: Okay.

Mrs. O: And how are you doing?

Priscilla: Okay, I guess, but I'm missing a quiz now (becoming nervous). Is that okay?

Reflection "in" Practice

Priscilla seems very nervous, and defensive. I need to place her at ease so that she's not worrying about being penalized for being here rather than in class.

Mrs. O: I knew you were having a "practice" quiz, but Ms. Elkin said that she was using this quiz as a review. She said that she was letting the class practice with the quiz so that students who may be having some difficulty might start to see where they need to work a little more. She told me that you know this section of the material really well. She said you got a 100 on the last two quizzes.

Priscilla: I did. I try to get 100s on everything. But what do I do now if I'm missing the quiz?

Mrs. O: Again, according to Ms. Elkin, you really don't need to take this quiz because it's on a lot of the material that you already got a 100 on. She said it would be okay if you came down and spoke with me today, rather than sit and take the practice quiz. Is that okay with you?

Priscilla: Yeah. I just don't want to get a bad grade.

Mrs. O: I understand that you are a very good student and I wouldn't do anything to hurt your grade, so we'll be fine for this period.

Priscilla: Are you sure (becoming nervous)?

Mrs. O: Yes, Priscilla, it is really just a practice quiz and Ms. Elkin said she wasn't even going to grade it. It is just to help the students feel a little more relaxed when they take quizzes. So, you really don't have to worry about missing it.

Priscilla: Okay.

Reflection "in" Practice

Priscilla is really locked into this quiz and her anticipation that somehow missing it will jeopardize her grade. I want to affirm her, but maybe start to challenge this reaction?

Mrs. O: Priscilla, you look a little upset. Are you okay?

Priscilla: I guess, but am I in trouble?

Mrs. O: Trouble? No, Priscilla, you are not in any trouble, not at all. Why would you think you are in trouble?

Priscilla: I don't know. I am not sure. Don't bad kids come to the counselor's office?

Reflection "in" Practice

I can see what Ms. Elkin is concerned about. Priscilla seems overly concerned about her grades and about being in trouble. She presents as being very anxious. She seems to be projecting that danger in some form is looming in her future, whether it be missing the practice quiz, or being in trouble. I need to go slow and be as affirming and supporting as possible. I don't think any challenging would be useful at this point. I need to be sure not to prematurely confront her or else she may process my response as a rejection and a sign that she did something wrong.

Mrs. O: Oh, I can understand why you may be nervous. If it was true that only children who are bad and in trouble came to see me, and then wow, here you are ... then I would surely understand why you might think that you were in trouble. Yep, I guess if a school counselor only talked to students who were in trouble then it would make sense to predict that you must be in trouble since I called you down.

Priscilla: Yes, but am I?

Mrs. O: No, Priscilla, honestly, you are not in trouble, not even a little bit, and I am really sorry that I didn't explain that to you when we first sat down. I certainly don't want you feeling worried or upset or afraid that you are here.

Priscilla: Okay.

Reflection "in" Practice

Maybe I can use this to start introducing the concept of the thought-feeling connection.

(Continued)

(Continued)

Mrs. O: I really should have explained that as the school counselor I talk to most of the children here at school. Sometimes students will come because they got in some trouble, you know, like maybe they got into an argument with another student, or maybe broke one of the school rules. But a lot of the students I talk to just come down to tell me about things that they have been doing, you know, maybe went on a vacation or joined the school chorus, those kinds of things. Some of the students I see just come in to talk about their friends or hobbies. Sometimes students will come down to talk to me because they are feeling a little sad about something that has happened or even a little nervous or worried about something. So, you see, I talk to a lot of students and most of them are not in trouble. Does that help you to relax a little?

Priscilla: Yeah.

Mrs. O: Oh, I'm glad. I'm sorry that I didn't explain that when we first got together, because I can see that if you thought that I spoke to lots of people about all kinds of things, then you wouldn't have made yourself as nervous as you did when you thought I only spoke to students who are in trouble.

Priscilla: Yeah, I was afraid 'cause I didn't know what I did wrong.

Mrs. O: And now?

Priscilla: I think I know why I'm here.

Mrs. O: You do?

Priscilla: Yes, because Ms. Elkin always tells me I have to relax. She says I have to relax, stop worrying. She says that I'm too nervous and I worry even when there is nothing to worry about.

Mrs. O: So, she thinks you may worry too much about things that really are nothing to worry about? How does that make you feel?

Priscilla: I don't know. My mom and dad say that too.

Mrs. O: They do?

Priscilla: Yeah. I sometimes get upset if I have trouble with a game or I can't do something.

Mrs. O: Hmm. So, a couple of people, people who really care about you—you know, your teacher and your mom and dad—say things like, "Priscilla you need to chill...you need to relax...you are doing fine...there's nothing to worry about" (smiling). Does that sound right?

Priscilla: Chill (laughing)...that's what my brother always says.

Reflection "in" Practice

Priscilla seems to be relaxing and less defensive at this point. I know we haven't gotten to her anxiety around the academic issues, but maybe the relationship is strong enough and supportive enough to begin to introduce the thought-feeling connection.

Mrs. O: Chill. Sounds right, but sometimes it's easier said than done?

Priscilla: I don't know why I get so nervous.

Mrs. O: Well, you don't seem nervous right now?

Priscilla: I'm not. I like talking with you.

Mrs. O: And I like talking with you. But I'm wondering. When you first came in, you seemed kind of nervous and upset and now you are not. What do you think changed?

Priscilla: I thought I was in trouble and I was worried 'cause I didn't know why or what was going to happen.

Mrs. O: Oh, and thinking that you were in trouble made you nervous?

Priscilla: Yeah.

Mrs. O: And now? You are less nervous. Why?

Priscilla: I guess 'cause we have been talking about me learning to relax.

Mrs. O: Chill (smiling)?

Priscilla: Yeah, chill (smiling).

Mrs. O: So, the thing that has helped you to relax in here is simply that you changed the way you were thinking from "I'm in trouble" to something like, "This isn't bad. Mrs. O'Malley just wants to help me learn to relax." Does that sound right?

Priscilla: Yeah, I guess.

Mrs. O: Priscilla, I know you want to get back to class, but I would love to see you again. I bet if we could figure out what you are thinking during those times when you are getting upset, maybe we could help you to think something else that would help you relax . . . chill? Would you be okay coming down and talking with me?

Priscilla: Yeah, I'd like that.

Mrs. O: Great. I'll check with Ms. Elkin and see if there is any time coming up when she would be working with the students who need a little extra

(Continued)

(Continued)

> help in their schoolwork, and you could come here rather than stay in class and do silent reading. How does that sound?

Priscilla: Okay.

Reflection "on" Practice (Following the Session)

I feel really good about that session. I wanted to establish a working relationship and I think I did. I wanted to test my hypothesis that Priscilla has a tendency to jump to somewhat catastrophic conclusions, which in turn make her very anxious and I think I saw a couple examples of that type of thinking. I also feel good about at least laying a foundation for helping her to see the thought-feeling connection, which is where I want to go with her the next time we sit. For now, I need to get back to Ms. Elkin and thank her for the referral and see when I can call Priscilla back down.

Session 2: Helping the Student Understand and Embrace the Thought-Feeling Connection

We pick up the interaction after the initial exchanges, after which Priscilla shared with her parents her excitement about talking with the counselor and her understanding that they were going to help Priscilla "chill" (relax) more.

Mrs. O: And when you are not chilling, what are you doing? Or how are you feeling?

Priscilla: I don't know . . . I get nervous.

Mrs. O: Priscilla, when you are nervous, how does that feel?

Priscilla: I get a funny feeling in my stomach, and I sometimes cry and feel like I want to run away and hide.

Mrs. O: Is that kind of how you felt when you first came here?

Priscilla: Yeah, I thought I was going to cry when you told me to come.

Mrs. O: So, when you first came to the office, you were feeling nervous, kind of scared, like the funny feeling in your tummy and feeling like you may want to cry? And when you first came in feeling that way, do you remember what you were thinking was going to happen?

Priscilla: I was worried I was in trouble.

Mrs. O: And you were worried that you were in trouble because?

Priscilla: I was in the counselor's office.

Mrs. O: You mean my office made you afraid?

Priscilla: No. I thought I was in trouble.

Mrs. O: Oh, okay. That's right. You thought only bad kids, or kids in trouble, came here. So if you were here, then I guess that must have meant . . . ?

Priscilla: I was in trouble because I did something bad.

Mrs. O: So, it wasn't my office that made you nervous, but the fact that you really believed that you were in trouble?

Priscilla: Uh-huh.

Mrs. O: And that belief that you were in trouble is because you thought only bad kids come to the counselor?

Priscilla: Uh-huh.

Mrs. O: Hmm . . . so just thinking that something bad is going to happen, even when it isn't, can make you feel really afraid?

Priscilla: I guess. I was really afraid.

Mrs. O: I am sorry to hear that, and I'm glad you are no longer afraid to be here and talk with me, but I guess what I am really happy about is that you are no longer thinking things to make yourself afraid.

Priscilla: No. I like coming here.

Mrs. O: That's great. But Priscilla, isn't it kind of wild how our thinking can really get us all scared and thinking bad things? But, I guess in one way, that's good to know, because if it is our thinking that is making us feel so afraid, then that means we can stop feeling afraid just by thinking differently.

Priscilla: I guess?

Reflection "in" Practice

She's being polite, but I can see she still doesn't get it. I need to break it down a bit more, get more concrete in my presentation.

Mrs. O: Well, think about it. Here you are in the counselor's office, and nothing bad has happened and you are not in trouble, but you were feeling really nervous and scared before you came. Are you feeling nervous and scared now?

Priscilla: No (smiling).

Mrs. O: But what's different? It's the same counselor's office and I'm the same counselor. So how come you were afraid before and not now?

Priscilla: 'Cause I'm not in trouble.

Mrs. O: Bingo! That's what I meant. When you believed you were in trouble, that belief, that thought, made you get very worried. But now you believe that you are not in trouble and you didn't do anything wrong. And now, how do you feel?

(Continued)

(Continued)

Priscilla: Okay.

Mrs. O: Yep, okay. And the reason for that is that you believe everything is okay.

Priscilla: But when I have to do school stuff that's different. Those things make me scared.

Reflection "in" Practice

I think Priscilla started to see the connection of thought to feeling as it applies to coming to the office, but she is clearly having difficulty applying this to the issues of classroom tasks and achievement. She seems comfortable with me, so maybe I could get her to work through a specific academic issue and maybe concretely represent it in a column format.

Mrs. O: Well, I have an idea. Let me write some things down on this piece of paper and maybe we can see if it is the school stuff that Ms. Elkin gives in class that makes you so nervous, or if it is the way you think about those tests and assignment that makes you nervous.

Priscilla: Ah (appearing confused).

Mrs. O: Priscilla, this isn't real easy to understand, but I'm really impressed by how you are following along, so maybe you could give me an example of a time when you felt really nervous in class?

Priscilla: You mean like yesterday? We had to color in the capitals of all the states and then hand that in so that Ms. Elkin could hang them in the room.

Mrs. O: That sounds neat.

Priscilla: It was fun, but Ms. Elkin told us to hand it in, and I wanted to check my answers again, but she wouldn't let me keep it longer and check to make sure I had them all right. She made me hand it in and I was really scared and I started to cry.

Mrs. O: I'm sorry you were so upset. But maybe we can figure some things out that will help you not feel so afraid or upset when things like this happen. Would that be okay?

Priscilla: Yeah, the kids thought I was a baby for crying. I didn't like that.

Mrs. O: Okay, well look here (pointing to a piece of blank paper). Let me write down what you just said over here (pointing to the first column on the sheet). I'm going to call this the "Real Event." This is the thing that happened in class. You know, it is what I would have seen happening if I were in the class. Now, if I understood what you said, you were feeling very upset and cried when Ms. Elkin said (using a "teacher voice"), "Okay class, pass your maps to the front."

Priscilla: Uh-huh (smiling).

Mrs. O: Okay.

Priscilla: And I tried to hold on to the paper and I started to cry and I said "Please, please let me check it."

Mrs. O: So, the real event was that we—remember I'm in class too—had to hand in our papers (miming the process of handing in a paper).

Priscilla: Yeah (smiling), and my map is better than yours (laughing).

Mrs. O: I bet you are right! I'm not very good at coloring. Okay, so I'll write that down. I'll write down that Ms. Elkin said to pass the maps to the front and everyone started to pass the maps, but Priscilla tried to hold on to hers and work some more. Now, you also said that you were really upset and cried. I will write that down over here (pointing to a third column). Let's call this column "Feelings and Actions."

Priscilla: Okay.

Mrs. O: And I am writing, "felt very afraid and started to cry." Is that how you felt?

Priscilla: Yeah, really afraid.

Mrs. O: Oh, okay. Let's change that to "really afraid." Now, here's what I'm wondering. You handed in your map and got very upset (pointing to the Real Event column). Now I handed in my map too; remember I'm in class. So, if handing in a map to Ms. Elkin was the thing that actually made you afraid and cry, then how do you think I would feel and act when I handed in my map?

Priscilla: I don't know.

Reflection "in" Practice

Probably a bad choice—my "presence" in the classroom is too unrealistic. I need to use a more realistic, concrete illustration.

Mrs. O: Well, I guess that's silly. I'm not in your class. But how about the other kids? They were handing in their maps so I guess they were all afraid and crying?

Priscilla: No, I was the only one (looking down).

Mrs. O: But they were all doing the same thing as you, you know, handing in the map to Ms. Elkin and yet they weren't feeling afraid or crying. Hmm, so I guess it wasn't handing in a map that made you feel that way?

Priscilla: I was the only one acting like a baby (looking sad).

(Continued)

(Continued)

Reflection "in" Practice

I need to slow down a bit. She's into the event and putting herself down about the crying. I need to reengage her in a way that enables her to feel empowered.

Mrs. O: Well, I don't think being afraid and crying means that you, or anyone for that matter, is a baby. But you know what? You just helped me.

Priscilla: I did?

Mrs. O: Yep. I mean, you are sure you were the only one, right?

Priscilla: Uh-huh.

Mrs. O: Hmm, just you . . . boy, now we can get somewhere (smiling). You did great!

Priscilla: I did?

Mrs. O: Yep. See, over here, we have the real event written down, and then we have your feelings and actions. I was just about to draw a line connecting these real events to your feeling but you just stopped me.

Priscilla: I did?

Mrs. O: Yep! Look. If I tried to connect these two things (pretending to draw the line), then it would mean that any time anybody, you know all the kids in your class, experienced those real events, then they would be afraid and crying . . . all of those students handing their maps . . .

Priscilla: You too (smiling).

Mrs. O: Yep, me too. We would all be feeling those same feelings but we didn't. Now, if I add one more piece to this puzzle . . . right here (pointing to a middle position between the previously written columns) and I call this "stinkin' thinking" (smiling), maybe we can figure out what happened. Maybe you were doing something that no one else was doing?

Priscilla: You mean crying?

Mrs. O: Well, you were doing that, but I'm wondering if you did something else that actually caused you to cry?

Priscilla: Like what?

Mrs. O: Maybe some . . . stinkin' thinking (smiling)?

Priscilla: Stinkin' thinking (smiling)?

Mrs. O: I know that sounds silly, but for me, stinkin' thinking is any time I have a thought that gets me really upset about something when, in fact, there is nothing to be upset about. It's like the thinking that you were in trouble when you first came here. That was stinkin' thinking. I mean, it made you afraid and it wasn't true!

Priscilla: Yeah, stinkin' thinking.

Mrs. O: So, if you and I could hear what you were saying to yourself when Ms. Elkin said (speaking again in exaggerated teacher voice), "Okay class, pass your maps to the front," what did you think? What did you hear? What do you think you were thinking?

Priscilla: I don't know.

Reflection "in" Practice

Priscilla is really a sharp kid and is following me, but this is tough to understand, especially when one is so concrete in her thinking. Maybe a role play would help?

Mrs. O: Let's pretend that we are in class and I'm Ms. Elkin, and it's yesterday and you are just finishing your map. Can you tell me what you were doing?

Priscilla: I was finished and I was rechecking all the capitals. I wanted to make sure I got them all correct. I wanted to go back one more time and then I had to hand the map in.

Mrs. O: Okay. I want you to start to describe that again, but this time, I'm going to act like Ms. Elkin and tell you to pass the maps forward. When I do that, I want you to tell me what you are saying to yourself inside your head. Okay?

Priscilla: I don't know if I can do that.

Mrs. O: That's okay. We'll try it and see what happens. I'm not sure I'm going to be a very good Ms. Elkin (smiling).

Priscilla: Okay.

Mrs. O: So tell me what was happening?

Priscilla: I was finished and I was checking all the capitals. I wanted to make sure I got them all correct. So I was checking and then I wanted to go back one more time and . . .

(Continued)

(Continued)

Mrs. O: "Okay students, pencils, pens, and crayons down. Pass your map up to the front...hurry now...no need to check...just pass it up. Priscilla, it's time to pass up your map." Priscilla, what was your thinking as you heard me say, "Pass the map up." What were you saying to yourself?

Priscilla: I didn't want to.

Mrs. O: Okay, why not?

Priscilla: I may have some wrong.

Mrs. O: Okay. But what would that mean? Let's pretend you didn't get them all correct, then what?

Priscilla: That would be horrible. My parents would be angry, and everybody would think I was dumb (starting to get upset).

Reflection "in" Practice

I know she is getting upset, but I think she's fine, and we have a few more minutes and I think this is a great "teaching moment." I want to get her to test this thinking, about her mom and dad being angry. Try to help her separate the real issue from her imagined consequence.

Mrs. O: It's okay, Priscilla. You know, I can see why that may make someone really upset, but you are being a really big help to me, today. Remember I was trying to figure out why you would get so upset when your teacher just said, "Pass the map forward," even when the other students weren't upset and now I think I understand (writing in the middle column labeled "Thinking"). Look here (pointing to the paper), when you had to hand in the map without checking your answers one more time, you thought something like, "I am going to get some wrong and that would be horrible because my parents would be angry with me and everybody would think I'm dumb." Does that sound like something you may have been thinking and saying to yourself?

Priscilla: Yeah (getting upset).

Mrs. O: Wow. I bet if that was true, that your parents would be really angry with you for making a mistake, then something like that would make you scared. But I'm wondering, have your parents been angry with you in the past for getting grades lower than 100?

Priscilla: No.

Mrs. O: Hmm. Okay, so your parents haven't gotten angry with you, but you were still thinking that they would be?

Priscilla: I guess.

Mrs. O: Well, that seems to be what went through your mind when we were role playing, so I guess I want to check it out to see if it's true. I mean, are you sure your parents wouldn't be angry with you?

Priscilla: I know they wouldn't. My parents tell me just as long as I try my best, they will be happy with any grade I get.

Mrs. O: So, the truth is that your parents wouldn't be mad, but for some reason, you seemed to have forgotten that and instead told yourself that they would really be mad. Now that sounds like stinkin' thinking (smiling).

Priscilla: Yeah, like when I thought you were going to be mad with me when I came here (smiling).

Mrs. O: Priscilla, that's right on. You're the best. That stinkin' thinking made you afraid to come here, even though you didn't have to be afraid because nothing bad was going to happen, and now you are thinking something bad will happen if you get something wrong on the map, yet nothing bad will happen. Yep. You got it. That's stinkin' thinking! I wonder what would have happened if, when Ms. Elkin said, "Pass up your maps," if you said to yourself something like, "Oh, well. I did the best I could. I hope I did okay, but either way, my parents will be proud I tried." I wonder if you were saying that to yourself, how you would have felt?

Priscilla: I guess okay.

Reflection "in" Practice

I think we are close, but she still seems to be a bit unclear about this. Maybe I could try something a little less personal in illustrating the thinking-feeling connection. I wonder if that would reduce her own defensiveness about this situation.

Mrs. O: Priscilla, you know what? You are really doing a super job trying to understand how our stinkin' thinking can upset us. But, I'm wondering if before we stop, I could show you something. I bet this is something that even your mom and dad may not know and something you could teach them. Okay?

Priscilla: Okay (becoming excited).

Mrs. O: Let me write down a different event over here (using the same sheet of paper with the three columns listing "Events," "Thinking," and "Feelings"). This time, let's pretend that you and I are babysitting for a little child, someone about three- or four-years-old.

Priscilla: My brother is almost four.

(Continued)

(Continued)

Mrs. O: Great. So, let's pretend we are babysitting your brother and it's time to put him to bed. We get him in his room and you know it's nighttime, so it's dark, and let's make it a rainy night so it's a little windy and noisy. Okay?

Priscilla: Okay (looking as Mrs. O writes the description of the situation in the first column).

Mrs. O: Well, in about five minutes, your brother starts to cry really, really loudly and we go into his room and he's sitting up and really afraid (writing this down in the column under "Feelings"). Okay?

Priscilla: Yeah, my brother Thomas does that, and my parents have to go in and sleep with him until he falls back to sleep.

Mrs. O: I bet he is really afraid when that happens. But look here (pointing to the "Thinking" column). I bet if you and I could get into Thomas's brain as he was drifting off to sleep, and just as he heard a noise in the dark, I bet we would hear him say something like, "What's that?" (speaking in a soft voice). "What's that?" What do you think he thinks it is . . . pretend you hear his thinking . . . here he is in the dark hearing a noise and thinking, "What's that? Oh . . . what's that? It's a . . . ?"

Priscilla: Monster!

Mrs. O: Yeow! I bet you are right. And you know what? If there was a real monster in this room, I would be screaming . . . yeow.

Priscilla: Yeow (laughing).

Mrs. O: But is there?

Priscilla: No.

Mrs. O: So, if there is no monster in his room to make him afraid, and yet he is feeling really, really afraid, then it must be his thinking, his belief that there is a monster in the room, that is causing him to be so afraid. That's sad. I mean, he is really upset but there is no real monster to make him upset. It's just his own thinking that is upsetting him. No monster, just a silly thought—you know, some stinkin' thinking. Boy, if we could only help him to stop thinking there's a monster, he would stop feeling afraid?

Priscilla: Yeah.

Mrs. O: You know what? We all have times when we have stinkin' thinking and when we do, we make ourselves upset or angry or scared when we really don't need to be. So, I have an idea. How about if you and I try to listen to your thinking so that we can help you get rid of any stinkin' thinking that you may have? If we can do that, you know, stop silly thoughts, then you will stop feeling so afraid at times when you don't need to be afraid. Would that be okay?

Priscilla: You mean like when I was crying in class?

Mrs. O: Yep, that would be a good example, since it was what you were thinking, "Oh, boy. My parents will be really mad if I get less than 100" that was making you upset and yet when we think, really think, about how your mom and dad would be without that silly thought, we know what?

Priscilla: That they said it's okay if I try my best.

Mrs. O: Yep, and that's not a reason to be crying or so upset, right?

Priscilla: Right.

Mrs. O: So, maybe between now and Friday you could try to remember any time that you became really upset or afraid. And when we get together, you can tell me about what was really happening and maybe together we could figure out if there was any stinkin' thinking going on?

Priscilla: What if I can't remember (becoming anxious)?

Reflection "in" Practice

She's turning this task into a do or die test. I need to model a noncatastrophic approach.

Mrs. O: If you can't remember, no big deal. If you can't remember, I guess that means you are like me and your mom and dad and everyone else I know. We all forget! So, do your best and even if you don't remember one time you had stinkin' thinking, we'll figure something out. Okay?

Priscilla: Okay (sounding calm).

Mrs. O: Well, we have to get you back to class, but thanks for coming and I can't wait to see you Friday. In the meantime, no stinkin' thinking (smiling).

Priscilla: Okay, bye.

Reflection "on" Practice

What a neat kid! I really enjoyed talking with her; she's so sharp. I know that this is a tough concept for her, but I think she is going to get it. Next time, if she has some examples of situations in which she was upset, I will use those to explore the thinking. But even if she doesn't, maybe I could see how she feels about not having any examples and use that if she's worried. Worst case, I'll bring a little worksheet that we could do together to demonstrate the thinking-feeling connection and even some role play. Maybe we could draw some type of symbol for stinkin' thinking that she could use later to assess if her thoughts are distorted. I think I have enough strategies for now.

Postscript

The counselor in this situation continued to meet with Priscilla but decided to expand the effort by creating a little group including other second- and third-grade students exhibiting anxiety. She set the following goals for this closed end psycho-educational group: (a) teach the students the concept of the thought-feeling connection; (b) help them recognize stinkin' thinking as thoughts and self-talk that is not really supported by the evidence; (c) develop strategies to employ as "thought-stopping techniques"; and (d) employ a process she called "replace the stinkin' thinking," which helped the students develop thoughts that would be more reflective of the reality they were experiencing.

CASE 2: NATALIE

Background

Natalie is a tenth-grade student who comes to the counselor's office upset and tearful. Apparently, she and her boyfriend got into an argument at lunch and he suggested that maybe they should take a break from each other, and start to see other people. Natalie is clearly distraught and unable to calm herself enough to return to class. The case, as presented, is a "one-shot" opportunity and the counselor, Mr. Costello, attempts to make the most of this time together to not only support Natalie at this time of crisis, but also provide her some new insights and skills that will serve her well in the future if similar events are encountered. As Natalie starts to share the story, Mr. Costello is immediately aware of his own thoughts as he processes her story.

Reflection "on" Practice

I really need to balance myself and be sure that I don't "minimize" adolescent love or in any way discount Natalie's feelings. She is feeling really crappy. I want to support her, but be careful to act as if I agree that this break up is "factually" the end of the world. I know that's how it seems to her. Maybe I can allow her to tell her story and gently confront some of her perspective, her conclusions, with some gentle questioning?

Session 1: Focusing on Crisis

Mr. C: Natalie, it's okay, just sit and try to relax. Would you like some water?

Natalie: Okay (nodding).

Mr. C: Take your time (handing her a cup of water), and maybe you would tell me a little more about what went on at lunch. I know you said you and Anthony got into a fight. Could you tell me what happened?

Natalie: It was horrible (crying). We were sitting at the table and he started complaining about me calling him all the time. He said it was embarrassing and that I was becoming a pain…and….(breaking down, crying).

Reflection "in" Practice

I need to slow down. She needs to know I hear her and value what she is going through, but I also want to convey a message of hope, that we will work this out.

Mr. C: Take your time; it's okay (waiting as Natalie drinks more water and wipes her eyes). So, Anthony was upset about you calling and text messaging and he wanted you to stop or slow down? Is that right?

Natalie: I've screwed up. He's going to break up with me. This is horrible (crying).

Reflection "in" Practice

I know this is her perspective, but I wonder how much of this is factual? It might help if I could get her to describe the event rather than staying focused on her interpretations.

Mr. C: So, you feel Anthony is breaking up with you? Is that something he said?

Natalie: Well, he didn't say that, but I know he's going to.

Mr. C: Oh, so he didn't say that, but you feel, you believe, that's what he meant? You believe that's what he intended?

Natalie: Yeah (starting to cry again).

Reflection "in" Practice

She's having a tough time refocusing on the "what is," and is clearly jumping to conclusions that are very upsetting. I want to bring her back to the actual event so that we can assess real consequences and decide how she can adapt to these. But I need to take it slow!

Mr. C: Natalie, I know you are upset and the situation seems really bad, but maybe if you could help me understand exactly what went on…maybe it would help?

Natalie: Okay (calming down).

(Continued)

(Continued)

Mr. C: I know you said that Anthony was upset, and that he was specifically upset about the number of times you called him and text messaged him, but I'm not sure what it is that leads you to conclude that he wants to end the relationship?

Natalie: I couldn't live without him (starting to cry).

Reflection "in" Practice

I think I need to risk being a bit more confrontational and directive to get her to focus. I also need to check that last statement of not being able to live without him. I need to be sure it is simply a dramatic statement and not a reflection of her level of despondency.

Mr. C: Natalie, I can tell this is very, very upsetting. But, I'm worried when I hear you say that you "couldn't live without him." Do you really mean that?

Natalie: No, but I really love him and I don't want the relationship to end.

Mr. C: Yes, I'm sure you really care about him, but I am concerned that you are upsetting yourself about the end of this relationship and yet we don't even know if that's true? Do we?

Natalie: No, not really. But he was really angry.

Mr. C: Okay, so he was angry, and when people are angry they sometimes say and do things that they wished they hadn't. What did he say or do that would give you evidence that he was ending the relationship?

Natalie: Well, he told me to cool it.

Reflection "in" Practice

She seems to be calmer, more focused. I think I can get her to see the power of her assumptions and help her attack some ill-founded thinking. Let's start by clarifying the "what is."

Mr. C: Oh, okay, and "cool it" meant what, exactly?

Natalie: Well, we were talking about the text messaging during class. I guess he meant cool it with the phone stuff.

Mr. C: Oh, okay, so it was the phone stuff he wanted to stop or slow down? It wasn't cool the relationship?

Natalie: I don't know; it could be.

Reflection "in" Practice

Okay. She's right. It could be the relationship, but I have to help her see that it is a hypothesis, and something that we need to test rather than immediately accept as fact.

Mr. C: I guess you are correct. I mean, he could have meant cool the relationship, but we really don't know whether he did or didn't, do we? And if it is the relationship he is referring to, we don't exactly know what he meant by "cool it," do we?

Natalie: No.

Mr. C: Natalie, if we knew for certain that the only thing Anthony meant was that he wanted you to slow down on all the phone contact, how would that make you feel?

Natalie: I don't call or text him that much.

Mr. C: Okay. But if that's what he meant when he said cool it, do you think you would be so upset?

Natalie: No, but I guess I'd still worry a little that he was mad and I'd be frustrated, 'cause I like talking to him.

Mr. C: Okay, so if we knew that what Anthony was really saying was slow down on the phone contact, then you would probably feel frustrated?

Natalie: Yeah.

Mr. C: But you wouldn't feel horrible and upset and so tearful?

Natalie: No.

Mr. C: Hmm. But if you knew for a fact that Anthony wanted to end the relationship, then how would you feel?

Natalie: Horrible.

Mr. C: Horrible?

Natalie: I'd be really sad. I really like him.

Mr. C: Oh, okay. So if we knew the relationship was over, you would be really sad.

Natalie: Yeah.

Mr. C: But do we know which, if either, of these two things are possibly true? I mean, was he talking about reducing the phone contact or ending the relationship?

(Continued)

(Continued)

Natalie: I don't know.

Mr. C: I can see why not knowing, with absolute certainty, what he meant could be confusing, but it seems that when you walked in here, you had pretty much convinced yourself that it was a *fact* that the relationship was over, and believing that made you really upset.

Natalie: Yeah.

Mr. C: So, just thinking that the relationship is over was what was upsetting you, and that was a thought that we don't even know is true, do we?

Natalie: No. I need to talk to him about what he meant.

Reflection "in" Practice

She's calm and focused. Maybe we can focus on some "problem solving," and "data collecting" while introducing the thought-feeling connection.

Mr. C: Good for you. It seems that rather than upset ourselves over something that may or may not be true, we should try to find out what is really happening.

Natalie: Yeah. I guess it just caught me off guard and I kept thinking this is horrible, and if he doesn't love me, I'll have no one.

Reflection "in" Practice

I think our relationship is strong enough and she is calm and focused enough to confront her.

Mr. C: Wow, lady! I think you are doing it again!

Natalie: Doing it again?

Mr. C: Listen to what you just said. If he doesn't want to go steady, then you really believe that is evidence that you will have no one in your life who cares about you, or enjoys you, or wants to hang out with you?

Natalie: That does sound kind of stupid, doesn't it? I meant I wouldn't have a boyfriend.

Mr. C: Okay, that sounds more accurate, but boy oh boy, I think that is quite a different thing than not having anyone in your life. I know it wouldn't be much fun not having boyfriend—although I'm sure that some of your friends may disagree (smiling)? But, I can't imagine what it would be like to have absolutely no one in the whole wide world who cared about you. I imagine that would be really a tough one.

Natalie: You're right about my friends. Rosario is always on my case about the fact that I never hang out with her anymore. She'd be happy if I didn't have a boyfriend (smiling).

Reflection "in" Practice

So, she has other friends and the relationship with Anthony even has some "costs" or downsides. Maybe if she could see this, it would help her gain perspective. I think I can point this out and use it to teach her more about the effect of our faulty thinking.

Mr. C: It sounds like Rosario is a good friend.

Natalie: Yeah, we have been friends since first grade.

Mr. C: Well, there you go. Even if you and Anthony aren't going steady, we know at least you will have Rosario in your life so any thoughts about being *all* alone (speaking dramatically) just aren't true, are they?

Natalie: No.

Mr. C: Natalie, let me show you something (getting out a piece of paper). Here's a situation where you are feeling really upset, sad, worried, and crying uncontrollably (writing this down on the right side of the paper in the "Consequence" column).

Natalie: Yeah.

Mr. C: I felt so bad for you. But when I asked you what happened, you said (writing it down on the extreme left of the paper in the "Activating Event" column) that "Anthony and you had an argument at lunch and he said that he wanted you to cool it with all the phone calls and text messaging." Now, when I look at these things, I'm confused. I am having trouble understanding how a comment like, "Could you cool it with the phone stuff" (pointing to what was written on the paper) caused you to be so upset?

Natalie: I was just worried.

Mr. C: Yes, you really were. You really were worried and really feeling sad. But as we were talking, I started to realize that you took Anthony's words and action and then in your head, you began to interpret them. You know, you started giving them meaning and that's what seemed to be making you so upset.

Natalie: I don't know what you mean.

(Continued)

(Continued)

Mr. C: Do you know when something happens, I don't know, like someone drops her books in the hall and all her papers scatter, and as you turn and see everything go all over the floor, you might say to yourself, "Ouch, that stinks" or something like that, in your head?

Natalie: Yeah, all the time.

Mr. C: Super. Well, if I got into your head while you and Anthony were having this argument, I wonder if I would hear you saying things like, "This is horrible. I can't stand it. He's breaking up with me. If he doesn't love me, no one will ever love me" (writing them down in the middle of the previous notes). Those kinds of things?

Natalie: Yeah, exactly. That's what I was thinking.

Mr. C: Yep, and because that's what you were thinking, because that was what you believed was really happening, then you started to react to your *thoughts* about what was happening, rather than simply reacting to what *actually* was happening. You started to feel so terribly upset and tearful because of what you were saying in your head. You know, for you, at the moment, it wasn't just Anthony telling you to stop calling so much. It was everyone in the whole wide world telling you they no longer loved you.

Natalie: But it was upsetting.

Mr. C: Well, I'm sure it was, arguing with someone you care about can be an upsetting event, but if rather than simply seeing it as upsetting or undesirable, we see it as something that we truly could not "stand" or that it meant that for the rest of your life you would have no one in your life who cared about you, then I guess it would be more than upsetting . . . it would be, as you said, "horrible" and "unbearable."

Natalie: Uh-huh.

Mr. C: But Natalie, even if Anthony wants to end the relationship—something we have no evidence to support—but even if he did, does that really mean no one, no one ever, will love you or that you couldn't be happy on your own?

Natalie: I guess not . . . but it felt so horrible.

Reflection "in" Practice

Two steps forward, one step back. It's hard to embrace this thinking-feeling connection especially when the feelings are so real. She is using emotional reasoning, and simply concluding that if it feels horrible, it must have been. I need to help her understand the event and the feelings are real, but that the source is her mediating thought and not the direct result of the event.

Mr. C: I'm sure it did. I am sure it really felt horrible. Those feelings were real. But it felt horrible because you *believed* it was horrible. I know this is not easy to understand, but our feelings in situations like this are not the direct result of the event, they are the result of our ways of looking at these events. Look, we could take the same event, "Anthony arguing with you," but this time let's pretend you have been thinking about ending the relationship and maybe even a little interested in some other guy, but didn't want to hurt Anthony's feelings so you just hung in there with Anthony. Now, what would you be thinking if he said, "Natalie, I think we should break up"?

Natalie: I guess (smiling), I'd be saying, "Whew. That's cool. I'm off the hook. Now I can date . . . Eric."

Mr. C: Eric (smiling)?

Natalie: Oh, that's just a name (smiling).

Mr. C: Yeah (doubting tone, smiling). And, if you thought (writing it down), "Whew. Cool, now I can date . . . Eric," how would you feel?

Natalie: I guess I would feel okay, maybe even good, relieved.

Mr. C: Right. So, the same event, that is, Anthony saying, "Natalie, I think we should break up," can result in different feelings. And, if the same event can cause different feelings, what determines the feeling a person has? I mean if it is not the event that is directly upsetting you, it must be . . .

Natalie: The way you see it?

Mr. C: Exactly.

Natalie: But I don't want to break up with Anthony.

Reflection "in" Practice

I think she's following. But I want to make sure she understands the goal isn't necessarily to "feel good," but to develop accurate interpretations of what is actually going on so that we can feel and behave in ways that are more effective for our dealing with this reality.

Mr. C: I understand that you really don't want to break up with Anthony, so if in *fact* he was breaking up, something we don't even know is true, but if he is and if you believed it, you might have said to yourself something like, "Well I didn't expect this. This is disappointing. I really like being with Anthony, and I don't know what went wrong. It wasn't a perfect relationship but it was a good one. I'll guess I'll be single again and hanging out with my friends." If these were the types of thoughts you had, how do you think you would feel? And, what do you think you would do?

(Continued)

(Continued)

Natalie: I guess I'd feel pretty sad and I might ask him what happened. I'd prob- ably just stay in for a while. My friends would probably start to bug me to go out.

Mr. C: So (writing on the paper), here's this one event and it can result in three different reactions depending on how you interpret it. If you believed, "This is disappointing. I don't know what went wrong. I'm single again," then you feel sad and maybe inquire what happened. If you believed, "Whew, now I can go out with Eric," you would feel happy and relieved. And if you look at the situation and convince yourself that, "This is hor- rible and unbearable and for the rest of my life I will have no one to love," then you become a complete mess.

Natalie: Yeah, that's what I was doing.

Reflection "in" Practice

She's got it . . . at least at this moment!

Mr. C: And sadly, that's what was making you feel so "horrible." Now we could sit here and try to convince you that he isn't breaking up, or that Eric is out there waiting (smiling), and I guess those thoughts would result in you feeling happy. Now I would love it if when you came in here I could help you go from being so very sad to being happy and joyful. But I think it is more beneficial if I could help you learn to hear your self-talk, you know, the way you interpret things, and learn to hear when you are making things worse than they are and then more accurately interpret what is going on. It doesn't do you or me any good to always think things are wonderful if they really aren't. But if we exaggerate the seri- ousness of the problem, that's not good either.

Natalie: That's for sure (smiling).

Reflection "in" Practice

She's really with me. Let's push her to do a little reformulation of her thinking based on the evidence.

Mr. C: We need to see it as it is and then deal with it. So if we really could step back and look at what's going on, you know, if we could get a real, objective view of what happened, what do you think we would see about what's really going on and what the consequence may be?

Natalie: I know what he said, but I really don't know what he meant.

Mr. C: That's a super start. And he said?

Natalie: That he really wanted me to "cool it" with the phone calling and text messaging during school.

Mr. C: Okay. So, that's the actual, real, objective event…was there anything else?

Natalie: Yeah, I don't know what he meant. I'm confused because I didn't think I was doing that much calling or texting.

Mr. C: So the event is that he said, "Cool it," but you are not sure what cool it really meant…and because you are unclear, you feel…?

Natalie: Confused.

Mr. C: Okay, and when you are confused about something, how do you act?

Natalie: I usually try to figure it out.

Mr. C: Okay, so what would you do to figure this out?

Natalie: I think I need to talk to him and find out what he meant.

Reflection "in" Practice

Fantastic. She's focused on taking some problem-solving steps, but I want to use this example to highlight the impact of thoughts on feelings and behaviors.

Mr. C: Super! That's amazing. When you jump to a conclusion that exaggerates the seriousness of the problem—you know, by believing this is horrible, you can't stand it, you will be left all alone for the rest of your life—you end up being devastated and having no way to solve the problem. But when you push yourself to just stick with the evidence, you know, just deal with what we know to be true, then the feelings we have seem to result in actions that help us in the situation. So, now you have something you can do to resolve your confusion. You can ask him what he meant when he said, "Cool it."

Natalie: Yeah.

Mr. C: Do you think you will be able to do that?

Natalie: Yeah, I'm okay. I can call him later, after school.

Mr. C: That's great. But remember, if you start to feel like it is horrible or unbearable, you have to get tough on yourself. Try to hear what you are thinking and try to challenge yourself to stick to the facts. Okay?

(Continued)

(Continued)

Natalie: I'll try.

Mr. C: You know, if you are having a little problem with that tonight, you could try writing it down like I did (handing her the paper with the Event-Belief-Consequence notes), and maybe even imagine you and I are debating your silly thoughts?

Natalie: That may help. Could I come down tomorrow and tell you how it went?

Mr. C: That would be a great idea. Why not stop down during third study? I'll tell Mr. Janson that you'll be with me tomorrow.

Natalie: Great.

Mr. C: How do you feel about going back to class?

Natalie: I'm okay. I'll just go to the bathroom first.

Mr. C: Hang in there, and I'll see you tomorrow.

Reflection "on" Practice

I am glad she came down. Clearly, she was able to calm down and regain her focus. I know she wanted to get back to class. She seemed to understand the thinking-feeling connection, but I'm sure it will be tough keeping her perspective if things go poorly tonight. When I see her tomorrow, I want to invite her to process her experience focusing on separating what "is" from what she "believes" is or what she believes it means. I don't want to make light of the hurt and anxiety that she feels, but I do want to help her to remove it from the category of the "horrible," "catastrophic," and "unbearable."

Session 2: Brief Encounter

Mr. C: Well? How are you doing?

Natalie: I'm okay, but things with Anthony, hmm, not so good.

Mr. C: Oh, I'm sorry to hear that. Want to tell me what happened?

Natalie: Sure. I called him and we talked a long time. It went okay, but the bottom line is he still wants to go out together but he just doesn't want to be exclusive or go steady.

Mr. C: How do you feel about that?

Natalie: I was kind of a mess last night, but I'm okay, now. It's funny. After talking with Anthony, I was like really the drama queen, crying and getting all crazy, and so I called Rosario to kind of cry on her shoulder. Boy, did she give it to me.

Mr. C: Give it to you?

Natalie: Yeah, as we were talking, she kept reminding me of all the things I had been complaining about because Anthony and I were going steady.

Mr. C: Complaining?

Natalie: Yeah, she was reminding about how I was complaining that I didn't have time to hang out with her and Akira, or how I didn't go to Ralph's party because Anthony doesn't like Ralph, that kind of stuff.

Mr. C: Hmm, so Rosario was kind of giving you evidence that some of your thinking about how horrible it would be without Anthony was not exactly accurate?

Natalie: Was she ever ... she was sounding like you (smiling).

Mr. C: I hope she doesn't take my job (smiling).

Natalie: Right (smiling).

Mr. C: So, it seems like even though you really liked Anthony, there was some downside to going steady?

Natalie: Yeah, that's kind of what Rosario and I decided. You know, he's cool and I really like him and like going out once in a while, but maybe I should not be going steady with anybody. It's just too ... too (searching for a word).

Mr. C: Restrictive?

Natalie: Yeah, restrictive.

Mr. C: Well, after you spoke with Rosario, how did you feel?

Natalie: I was okay, in fact I went downstairs and hung out with my family and actually had a good time just relaxing with them.

Mr. C: That's great. Do you have an explanation for how your talk with Rosario helped?

Natalie: I don't know (smiling), maybe just recognizing that I was missing out on some things and that I had a bunch of friends to hang out with helped me see it wasn't the end of the world.

Mr. C: Fantastic! So, the things Rosario was pointing out really made it hard for you to think that this was the end of the world, that it was horrible and unbearable, and that no one would ever love you?

Natalie: Yeah. In fact, I was writing down all the things she and I were talking about, just like you did and it really helped (showing her notes).

(Continued)

(Continued)

Mr. C: Natalie, that's super. It seems that keeping your thoughts focused on what really was happening and preventing yourself from exaggerating, or what I call "catastrophizing" the situation, really helped you feel okay?

Natalie: Yeah, it really did. I'm going to remember to do this any time I start to become a drama queen.

Mr. C: Good for you! That sounds like a great idea.

Natalie: Yeah.

Mr. C: Well, that's the bell, so if you are okay, you probably should get back to class.

Natalie: Yeah, I have a chem test next period.

Mr. C: Chemistry? Well, good luck, stay focused, and even with the test, "no catastophizing" (smiling)!

Postscript

Mr. Costello saw Natalie later that day and simply asked how the chemistry test went. Her response was, "Not good, not bad … but absolutely not a catastrophe." Her comment, along with her little smile, made him feel that the interaction was certainly profitable and Natalie was a girl who had regained her perspective.

FINAL THOUGHTS

In the final chapter, Chapter 7, you will once again be provided a case illustration. However, this time, in addition to observing a school counselor operating with a cognitive orientation, you will be invited to participate in the reflective processes occurring throughout the sessions.

At various points in the case presentation, you will be asked to reflect on what is happening as well as what it is that you would do next in the process. The hope is that by stepping into the dialogue, you will be able to translate your understanding of the cognitive model into its application.

Practice in Procedural Thinking

7

T he previous chapter presented examples of two counselors employing a cognitive orientation to guide their reflections on the material being presented and their decisions in response to those data. The cases illustrated the counselors' procedural thinking as they responded to the material and information provided by each student. The current chapter invites you to move beyond simply observing the procedural thinking of a counselor with a cognitive orientation, to actually engaging in that very process.

This final chapter provides the case of Randall. It is a case that illustrates a process of moving from the initial "hello" through to termination. As you read the case material, you will note places where the counselor, Ms. Schulman, reflects on the material gained in practice and uses that reflection to guide her decisions and actions. However, prior to viewing Ms. Schulman's reflections and decisions, you will be invited to use a cognitive-oriented framework or lens through which to process the same student data being presented and anticipate the counselor's response. It is hoped that with this type of practice in anticipating the counselor's response, you will move from understanding the concepts and constructs of cognitive theory to employing a cognitive framework to guide your own reflective practice.

One final note to consider prior to presenting the case is that this case of Randall, the sixth-grade bully, is employed in the companion texts within this series. The reason for this replication is that it will provide readers the opportunity to compare and contrast the variations in reflections and practice of a school counselor as she employs a variety of orienting frameworks to guide her practice decisions.

RANDALL: THE SIXTH-GRADE BULLY

History and Context

Tammy Schulman is the middle school counselor at E. L. Richardson Middle School. Ms. Schulman receives a referral from the assistant principal that reads:

> *Tammy, I've been hearing numerous complaints from teachers and students about Randall Jenkins. While we are only three weeks into the school year, Randall has already accrued ten demerits for fighting. It is clear that unless we do something, Randall won't be here by midterm. Please see him as soon possible.*

Reflection "on" Practice

Assuming you are a school counselor with a cognitive orientation, what would you do upon receiving this referral?

Ms. Schulman does not know Randall, so she wants to see if there are any data in his cumulative folder that would suggest possible explanations for this behavior and strategies that may have been used by his previous counselors. Ms. Schulman discovers very little information in the folder.

Randall was a recent transfer to E. L. Richardson and his previous school had yet to send relevant files. However, what Ms. Schulman does discover is that Randall is new to the district having moved here with his mother following his parents' divorce. As Ms. Schulman sits waiting for Randall to come down in response to her request to see him, she reflects on what she is hoping to accomplish as a result of this initial meeting.

Reflection "on" Practice

If you were the school counselor in this situation and operating from a cognitive frame of reference, what goals might you have for this initial session and how might you go about achieving these?

As Ms. Schulman sits at her desk, she jots down a couple of reminders: "relationship before resolving," "develop a working alliance," "show support," and "invite his story." It is clear from her notes that she values the counseling relationship and the need to "hear" Randall's worldview. She assumes Randall has an explanation for his behavior—an explanation that may likely place the responsibility on forces outside of himself.

Session 1: Building a Working Alliance

Ms. S: Randall, come in, and thanks for coming, I'm Ms. Schulman, the sixth-grade counselor.

Randall: (Looks down, and sits without talking.)

Ms. S: Randall, do you know why I asked you to come down and see me?

Randall: (Still looking down, and shows little response.)

Ms. S: Randall, you look a little uncomfortable, are you mad at me for some reason?

Randall: (Looks up, somewhat surprised by the question.)

Ms. S: Thanks for looking up. I wasn't sure if I was doing something wrong, because you look really unhappy. Are you unhappy right now?

Randall: (Nods yes, still not talking.)

Reflection "in" Practice

As a counselor working from a cognitive orientation, how do you interpret and respond to Randall's initial presentation?

    Looking at Randall, Ms. Schulman "feels" as if he is building a self-protected buttress—arms crossed, chin on his chest, looking down, and showing minimal responses. Her read is that he is preparing for an assault and is clearly being defensive. With this interpretation, she feels that she needs to demonstrate support and encouragement, and invite Randall to set the direction for the session. She feels that the "problem" can wait and that what is needed is special attention to the development of a working alliance.

Ms. S: Randall, I am really sorry that you are unhappy. I wish I could help. You know, I am really amazed that even with you being this unhappy, you were still able to come down here and meet with me.

Randall: I had to come. You sent for me.

Ms. S: Yes, I guess that is correct, but you did come and I appreciate that you did, and really appreciate you talking with me now.

Randall: Yeah, okay.

Reflection "in" Practice

Randall sounds angry. He has moved from the quiet, defensive posture to at least providing some minimal verbal response. At this point, sensing his immediate problem of being "unhappy" and apparently defensive, what might your next move be?

(Continued)

(Continued)

With Randall at least now showing some minimal willingness to engage verbally, Ms. Schulman wonders how he would respond to her invitation to discuss his feelings of anger and recent fighting behavior. She feels that she will have to go slow and not come across as accusatory or punitive or else he may shut down. In this case, she feels that building a working alliance takes precedence over engaging in the work of cognitive counseling.

Ms. S: Randall, you are correct in that I did want to meet with you. I was talking to Dr. Kim and he was telling me that you have had a problem with some of the other kids in school. I was hoping you would tell me a little about what has been going on?

Randall: It's not my fault (looking down).

Ms. S: It's not your fault? Okay . . . but what is the "it" we are talking about?

Randall: Fighting.

Reflection "in" Practice

Now that Randall has taken some ownership for "a" problem, what data would you like to gather and/or which direction would you like to take? At this early stage of counseling, what would your goals be, assuming you are employing a cognitive orientation?

Ms. Schulman hopes that now that Randall has introduced the idea of "fighting" that maybe she could use an illustration of a recent situation to begin to introduce the concept of the thinking-feeling connection. She knows that for someone Randall's age, a concrete illustration can facilitate the understanding of this concept.

Ms. S: Fighting? Hmm. . . . you know what? It would really help me if you could tell me about the fighting.

Randall: Like what?

Ms. S: Well, maybe you could tell me about a recent time when you got in trouble for fighting.

Randall: I was sent to Dr. Kim once because Boston and I were pushing each other in lunch line and then I went to Dr. Kim because Chuck Hammel and I got into an argument in the bathroom and then started pushing each other, until Mr. Allison stopped it.

Ms. S: Oh, so you had two recent situations, one with Boston, I assume you mean Ralph Boston, and one with Chuck Hammel. Hmm. Would you mind telling me a little more about one of these situations—maybe the one with Ralph Boston?

Reflection "in" Practice

While we are not sure if Randall will be able to accurately report on these incidents, what do you think Ms. Schulman may be looking for? Or how might she use these data? Assuming you were using a cognitive orientation, what would you do at this point in the interaction?

Ms. Schulman is hoping to use the situation with Ralph to demonstrate the A-B-Cs of a cognitive approach. She is aware of Randall's level of defensiveness and knows that while "challenging" his externalization of the problem, she needs to go slow and be sensitive to Randall's feelings.

Randall: Well, Boston just cut in front of me in lunch line and he said real loud so everybody could hear it, "What are you lookin' at, loser?" Then the other kids in line started making noises like "oooh" and saying things like "get him," that kind of stuff.

Ms. S: So Ralph just cut in front of you and called you a name, and then the other kids started to encourage you to do something?

Randall: Yeah, and then Boston, I mean Ralph, just kept lookin' at me and then said something like, "You want to do something about it, homo?" And then I got really angry and pushed him.

Ms. S: So, he called you more names and then you got really angry and pushed him. Would it be okay if I wrote that down?

Randall: I guess.

Ms. S: It will help me. Let me see if I understand it (starting to write down as she speaks). So you are in lunch line, and then Ralph jumps into line ahead of you and he makes this comment of "what are you lookin' at loser" and the other kids started to make noises. Is that pretty much the picture?

Randall: Yeah, he really made me mad, and I wanted to show him.

Ms. S: Okay, let me write that down over here. You said you were really mad and you wanted to show him, so you pushed him. Is that right?

Randall: Yeah, and I would have punched him if Mr. Jacobs didn't pull us out of line. He told us to go see Dr. Kim.

Ms. S: Hmm, okay. I think I got that. How about the other situation with Chuck?

Randall: It was after gym and I went to the bathroom and a couple of other guys from gym were in there and Chuck said real loud as I walked in, "Hey loser, who invited you?" and then everybody started to laugh.

(Continued)

(Continued)

Ms. S: So the other guys started to laugh? What happened next?

Randall: I was going to the stall and Chuck was going to the sink and he gave me a shove.

Ms. S: So he pushed you first?

Randall: Well, he kind of bumped me as we passed, but then he called me a name and the other guys started to yell "get him" and I just pushed him into the sink.

Ms. S: Oh, so he called you a name and then the other guys started encouraging you to do something and you pushed him?

Randall: Yeah, and that's when Mr. Allison came in and told me to go to Dr. Kim's office.

Ms. S: You know, in some ways, these two events are kind of similar. I mean, in both situations, it seems that the guys were calling you a name, like loser or something, and then the other students who were watching started to make noises and tell you to push him and things like that . . . and then you got very angry . . . hmm.

Randall: I guess (looking down). I kind of have a short fuse. But they really pissed me off—sorry.

Reflection "in" Practice

We now have two illustrations of Randall getting angry. How would you proceed? What would you like to accomplish before the end of this session?

Randall has taken some ownership over these incidents, but it is clear that he truly believes that his feelings and behaviors are "natural" reactions to the verbal teasing he experienced. While Ms. Schulman knows she can call him down to the office again, she really would like him to want to come back. She wonders if she can set up a little cognitive dissonance and use that as a motivation for him to want to come back so that they can resolve the conflict he may be experiencing.

Ms. S: Randall, that's okay. But I'm a bit confused. You seem like a pretty smart guy and so I'm confused as to why you would give these students so much power over you?

Randall: I don't give them anything. What are you talking about?

Ms. S: Well, if I understood what you said, it appears that you feel that the other students are the ones getting you in trouble?

Randall: I told you they piss me off (sounding annoyed).

Ms. S: I understood that is what you said, but that's exactly what I meant. If they really have the power to make you angry and get you in trouble, I guess I'm wondering why a guy like you hasn't decided to take that power back.

Randall: I don't get what you are saying.

Reflection "in" Practice

Cleary Ms. Schulman has stimulated some "confusion" in Randall. Where would you go at this point in the interaction? What do you anticipate she will do with this confusion?

Ms. Schulman feels she has stimulated curiosity and this may serve as a motivation to engage Randall in the counseling. Rather than simply addressing his behavior, she feels it is important to get him to begin thinking about his thinking and to find something of personal value in coming to counseling.

Ms. S: I have an idea. How about if I get you out of study hall tomorrow and I'll show you what I mean? I'll show you what it means to take the power back and then we can decide how to help you start taking that power back so that you won't get in trouble when the other guys try to make you mad. Okay?

Randall: I don't get it, but okay.

Ms. S: Okay . . . hang on, we'll figure it out. But for now, why don't you just think about it. See if you can figure out what I mean when I said, "giving the other students power." Okay?

Randall: Okay.

Reflection "on" Practice

It is clear that Randall is both confused and a bit curious. As you reflect on the session, and in anticipation of the upcoming session, what would be your goals for this next session? How would you build on his confusion over the issue of taking the power back?

As Ms. Schulman reflects, she concludes that while Randall was not as enthusiastic as she would like, he was at least open to coming back and coming back with his own issue rather than one that was imposed on him. She concludes that he is a bright guy and with his curiosity may be a great candidate for a cognitive approach. Her plan for the next session is to use the two situations that he described to illustrate the thinking-feeling connection and to play off the idea of him being in power to create or not create those upsetting feelings and behaviors.

(Continued)

(Continued)

Session 2: Shifting the Focus to the "Thinking-Feeling" Connection

Ms. S: Well, did you figure out what I meant?

Randall: No.

Ms. S: That's okay. I was a bit unclear. Let me explain. Yesterday, you gave two super examples of times when you got really angry and almost into a fight. And when you were describing these two events, you said that these other guys, Ralph and Chuck, made you mad.

Randall: Yeah, they did!

Ms. S: So, you seem to feel that they have this power, this ability to make you angry, and what I was suggesting is that they don't have that ability. In fact, I know that they don't have the power to make you mad—in fact, no one does, unless you give them that power.

Randall: I don't get it (looking confused).

Ms. S: Randall, you're not the only one, this is kind of wild. Watch. Have you ever been in a situation where someone has called you names and you just laughed or walked away and no matter what they were saying, it really didn't bother you?

Randall: You mean like when I'm playing basketball or baseball, something like that?

Ms. S: Maybe. Can you give me an example?

Randall: Yeah, like last week, I was pitching and the guys on the other team were trying to get me angry so that I would lose it and then I wouldn't be able to pitch.

Ms. S: How would they do that?

Randall: Well, they would yell things. I don't know, like, "Nice throw, spaghetti arm" or, "You call that a fast ball?" Oh yeah, the one I like and I am going to use on other pitchers was, "Didn't you play on the girls' soft-ball team?" and sometimes they say pretty bad things, but our coach doesn't let us do that.

Ms. S: Spaghetti arm (smiling)? Pretty creative. Now, would you get upset and loose your concentration when they did that?

Randall: No. I know they are trying to get me off my game so I just say to myself "focus," and then I pitch harder and if I struck one of them out I would just smile at their bench (smiling).

Ms. S: Cool. So, when you are on the field, you take the power back. I mean here are these guys calling you names…even some that are really bad, but you just keep thinking or saying to yourself "focus." And just thinking this helped keep you from getting all worked up? Is that how you do it?

Randall: Yeah.

Ms. S: That's cool. They had no power. Their words were just words, with no power.

Randall: Yeah. I knew what they were trying to do and so it didn't bother me.

Ms. S: So, you hear them say these things, and you just say to yourself, "I know what they are trying to do. I'm not going to let them get me upset. I'm just going to focus," or something like that?

Randall: Yeah, I guess.

Ms. S: Well, if thinking these thoughts helps you stay calm and keep the power, I wonder what you are thinking when the guys at school call you names? I mean, I wonder what thoughts you have that make you angry?

Randall: I'm not thinking anything. It's what those guys are saying that makes me mad.

Reflection "in" Practice

Randall is certainly engaged. He has given us some good material to work with. What do you do at this point, given his "retreat" to his early position that it is their words that cause the problem?

As Ms. Schulman reflects, she concludes that while he was following along, the reference to the school incidents seem too raw, and it stimulated his thinking that it was the external events that caused his reactions. She feels that he was engaged and connected enough in the counseling to begin to gently challenge/confront his thinking.

Ms. S: It probably seems like that. But Randall, it seems to me that if the name calling all by itself made you mad, then I wonder, wouldn't you be mad any time someone called you these names—even at the ball game?

Randall: I guess (sounding open yet not convinced).

(Continued)

(Continued)

Ms. S: I mean, there are some things, like if you touch a hot stove, that may cause a reaction—you know, pulling your hand away—but when that's the case, those situations always cause that reaction. You know, if you touch any hot stove, any time, any place, you will pull your hand away. But here's a situation where the same event, name-calling, gets different reactions. Hmm... so it doesn't seem to me that it is the name-calling that creates the anger.

Randall: But Boston and those guys really make me mad, so I have to show them, so I'll tell them to shut up or push them... or something.

Reflection "in" Practice

Randall provided a good illustration to contrast situations in which he responds to name-calling with anger and situations where he has no anger. But, the brief explanation by the counselor didn't appear effective. Randall may understand the connection but doesn't appear to own it. What would you do next?

Ms. Schulman realizes that Randall was following along with the "concept" and the "theory," but when it came to "owning" it on the personal level, he seems to be resistant. She feels that she needs to go a little slower and make the connection a bit more concretely.

Ms. S: Does that work?

Randall: Yeah.

Ms. S: Really? It works? To stop them from name-calling? Hmm, then why don't you just yell, "Shut up" on the baseball field during a game?

Randall: 'Cause they would just get worse and my coach would yank me, and besides, if I get that worked up, I can't pitch well.

Ms. S: Oh, okay. So, on the ball field, you getting angry and saying, "Shut up" wouldn't work because first, you would be too worked up, and then your coach may get annoyed and finally, the other team would just keep it up and even get worse. Hmm. But isn't that what is kind of happening here at school? I mean, you get so worked up in class that you are not doing as well as I know you could do, and then the teachers—you know, the classroom coaches—are getting annoyed with you and finally it seems that some of the kids just keep pushing your buttons, even more?

Randall: I guess.

Ms. S: So getting angry, upset, and pushing doesn't really seem to work, either on the ball field or here at school?

Reflection "in" Practice

What is your assessment of the degree to which Randall understands the thinking-feeling connection? What will you do next?

Ms. Schulman feels like she has Randall engaged. She feels that he is starting to understand what she was trying to illustrate in terms of the thought-feeling connection but he doesn't, at this stage, completely own it. She wonders if he needs to experience it rather than simply talk about it.

Ms. S: How about doing a little experiment for me?

Randall: Huh?

Ms. S: How about picking just one class from the rest of the day and as much as you can, try to pretend that it's a baseball game and you're pitching. So, no matter what any of the kids say, I would like you to remind yourself that they are trying to throw you off your game. I want you to say to yourself, "Relax and focus." Could you try that?

Randall: I guess. I have gym later, would that count?

Reflection "in" Practice

Randall is certainly more invested in the counseling than he was when they started. What is your plan for this mini-experiment? How will you use this experience in your next session?

Ms. Schulman feels like even if Randall hadn't fully embraced the thought-feeling connection, he certainly had become more engaged and active in the counseling. She reminds herself to really affirm him for even trying the mini-experiment and to go slow in analyzing his experience. Hopefully, the experiment will work, but even if it doesn't, she hopes to demonstrate that he lost his cool because he lost his "focus."

Ms. S: Gym? Super! That would be a good one, since you guys are out on the field. Maybe being outside will help you remember to keep thinking, "Stay in the game. Stay focused," and "Take the power back."

Randall: I'll try. I think I can do that.

Ms. S: Fantastic. Want to check in tomorrow during study hall?

Randall: Sure.

Ms. S: Okay. Stay focused (smiling).

(Continued)

(Continued)

> ### Reflection "on" Practice
>
> *It seems that Ms. Schulman has engaged Randall in the counseling process and has even provided him with an intervention to "stay focused." Assuming you are taking a cognitive orientation to working with Randall, what would your goals be for the next session?*

Ms. Schulman is happy with the direction the session took and feels that Randall is now engaged in the process. As she thinks about the upcoming meeting, she is mindful of the need to continue to support him and his engagement, to go slowly, and not elicit defensiveness, but hopefully use the homework as a concrete example to analyze in terms of the "power" of Randall's thinking.

Session 3: An "Ah, ha" Experience

Ms. S: Well? How did it go?

Randall: It was really cool.

Ms. S: Cool?

Randall: Yeah, we were playing softball in gym. Louis Marconi was pitching for our team and everybody was getting on him for throwing like a girl. Max Wilson really started getting into it. He was in the batting circle and saying, "Hey Marconi, do you wear a bra or what? My sister's got more strength in her arm and she's six-years-old." But then he gets up to bat and Marconi bounces the ball up to the plate and Wilson dropped to his knees and started laughing and then other guys started to whistle and Marconi just freaked out. He started screaming and went after Wilson. Mr. Afton had to come out and tell us all to get into the gym and he sent Wilson to Dr. Kim's office and had to tell Marconi to sit in his office and calm down. It was *crazy*.

Ms. S: I'm sorry to hear that. Wow, that was tough on Louis. Did Louis come back to class?

Randall: Yeah. He was okay. He just went ballistic, but he's fine.

Ms. S: That's good. But what did you mean when you said it was cool?

Randall: Marconi and the power thing.

Ms. S: Marconi and the power thing?

Randall: I mean, Wilson was just talking trash but Louis just kept getting himself all worked up.

Ms. S: Trash?

Randall: Well, Louis wasn't really pitching that bad and Wilson was just saying stupid stuff to get him upset. I kept thinking, "Focus, Marconi," but no way! He really was freaking himself out and it was stupid since Wilson was just playing with his head and his comments were dumb and there was no reason to get so freaky.

Reflection "in" Practice

What do you think? If you are taking a cognitive orientation, what do you plan to do with this insight that Randall is describing?

As Ms. Schulman listens, she thinks that Randall is starting to get the concept. Ms. Schulman feels that this is a good event to use as a focus point to begin to highlight the thinking-feeling connection. She assumes that since the issue is about another student, that Randall could be a bit more objective and actually see the connection of thought to feeling. So, her decision is to continue discussing and analyzing the event, seeing it as a teachable moment.

Ms. S: Fantastic! You got it.

Randall: Got it (smiling)?

Ms. S: Yep. You just showed me a great example of how we get ourselves all worked up, how we give the power away. But I bet Louis really believed it was Wilson making him angry.

Randall: Yeah, he wanted to kill Wilson.

Ms. S: It really is sad that he got that worked up, but as you saw, it was Louis who was actually doing it to himself. I mean, it was his thinking that was actually working himself up. Louis was actually making himself angry . . . not Wilson.

Randall: Yeah, it was really stupid.

Ms. S: I'm sure it didn't feel stupid. But you are right in one way. If Louis could have seen it as it actually was, you know, just some "dumb" words and nothing to really get angry over, then getting all freaked would seem silly . . . even to Wilson.

Randall: My dad told me that when he was a kid, they always said something like, "Sticks and stones can break my bones, but names can never hurt me!" He told me to remember that so that I wouldn't get all worked up when the other team talked trash.

(Continued)

(Continued)

Randall:	Well, your dad is right on. I mean, if someone is trying to hurt you physically, then maybe getting angry will help protect you. But when you get angry and act that way at times when there is no danger, that seems not very productive. I mean, here's poor Louis who is turning some silly, trash talking into danger. He's making himself feel that these dumb comments are really going to hurt him and he needs to get all worked up in order to defend himself. Isn't that sad?
Randall:	It was weird to see him freakin' over something so stupid.
Ms. S:	Yeah, but think about it. I bet he didn't think it was stupid. I mean, I bet it seemed real to him, you know, that this really was an attack that he had to defend himself against. I wonder, were any of the comments accurate? I mean, was Louis really that bad as a pitcher? And even if he was, does that make him a little girl?
Randall:	No, that's the weird thing. He was doing pretty good and striking guys out until he lost it!
Ms. S:	So, you are saying that all the things Wilson was saying were really not true in the first place, but Louis started to buy it and get himself all worked up, and then that screwed up his pitching and just made things worse?
Randall:	Yeah, cool huh?
Ms. S:	Well, I'd say interesting—interesting that our thinking can cause us to get really upset or angry or afraid, and then upset, and that can make us behave in ways that don't really work for us.
Randall:	Yeah, that's cool.

Reflection "in" Practice

Randall seems to see the connection of thought to feeling as it applies to Wilson and this one event. What would your goal be at this point in the interaction?

As Ms. Schulman listens, she thinks, "Wow, he's got it!" But, she knows that seeing the connection of thought to feelings is one thing, owning it as applied to one's own life is another. She wonders if the relationship is strong enough for her to turn the attention to Randall's own reactions when confronted with such teasing and "trash" talking. She decides to test it.

Ms. S:	Hmm . . . so, I'm wondering, Randall, do you think there are times when your thinking gets you all worked up in situations where you really don't need to be worked up?
Randall:	I guess you could say that (smiling).

Reflection "in" Practice

You "hear" the words and "see" the behavior... does Randall really get it? Do you push it?

As Ms. Schulman listens and observes, she thinks, "love that smile... got him!" She feels that the shy smile reflects an "ah, ha" experience where Randall sees the personal relevance and may even feel a little silly about being so silly as to give this much power to this type of teasing. She wants to support this insight, but also highlight that this is nothing to be ashamed of, and it is something that takes work to change.

Ms. S: That little smile seems to suggest to me that, "I got you" (smiling).

Randall: Maybe (smiling).

Ms. S: Yep. You, me, and everyone else we know can think in ways that really upset us, even when there is no real reason to be upset or worried or angry. But you know what, you and me are different than lots of other people, including Wilson, because we know the secret.

Randall: The secret?

Ms. S: Yep. We know that it's not what people say or do that *makes* us upset. It's what we think and say to ourselves about these events that can make us upset or not upset. You know, the same words said to you on the ball field can be seen as silly trash talk and then ignored, or we can make them life and death and get all worked up. It's not the words; it's the meaning we give to them... that's the secret!

Randall: Yeah, cool.

Ms. S: But you know what? It's not just the secret, but it's good news.

Randall: Huh?

Ms. S: Sure, I mean, if it's me doing this to me, you know getting me upset or the guys trying to throw me off my game, then I have the power!

Randall: You mean, like when I say, "Focus," that gives me the power to be calm and pitch.

Ms. S: Randall, you're the best... that's exactly it.

Randall: It is (smiling)?

Ms. S: But, just like we have the power to stay calm, we also have the power to freak ourselves out. So, we just have to figure out how we freak ourselves out and then stop doing it!

Randall: But how do we do that?

(Continued)

(Continued)

Reflection "on" Practice

Randall seems to get it, and even is starting to embrace it as a point of personal relevance. It might be time to move toward the next step of applying this insight to his own lived experience. As you prepare for the end of this contact, what would you hope to achieve and what homework, if any, might you try to introduce?

As Ms. Schulman listens, she feels that Randall is grasping the fundamental concept and his question about stopping it suggests that he is motivated to continue. As she thinks about the conclusion of this session, she wants to affirm his engagement, reinforce the concept of the thought-feeling connection, but then introduce the "work" that needs to be done to make this valuable to him and his current experience.

Ms. S: Great question. How about if we try a few things that can help you gain that power back, and use your thinking in ways that not only help you focus and stay in the game, but also help you stay calm and stay out of trouble at school?

Randall: What do I have to do?

Ms. S: Homework (smiling)!

Randall: No way (smiling).

Ms. S: Okay. Here's the deal (pulling out a piece of paper and making three columns on it). I would love you to take the rest of the week and weekend and keep a few notes for us. Here's what I would like you to do. If over the next couple of days you find that you are feeling angry or getting upset, I would like you to write down how you feel and just list it here (pointing to the third column, labeled "Consequence") and maybe how you were acting. For example, if we did it for Marconi, we would write (writing in the column), "Felt really angry and started to scream at everyone and threatening to punch Wilson." Got it?

Randall: So, could I say things like, "got pissed off and threw the bat"?

Ms. S: Yep. That's it. But then after doing that, I want you to describe what the actual event was, and jot that down over here (pointing to the first column, labeled "Event"). So again, if we use the situation at gym and we were doing this with Marconi, we would write, "I was pitching and Wilson started to call me a girl, and say I wore a bra and that his sister could pitch better than me and then he fell down and started laughing at me." That's actually what was happening.

Randall: I can do that, but then what? What goes here (pointing to the middle column)?

Ms. S: You are way ahead of me. Great job! Randall, you really are going to get that power back. So, okay, we know the name-calling wasn't what was making Marconi go ballistic. It was what he was thinking. So if you can, I want you to read what you wrote in the first column (pointing to "Event") and as you read it, try to "hear" what you are thinking, what you may be saying to yourself about the situation and just write all that down in this column. We'll call this column "Self-Talk" or "Thinking." Okay?

Randall: You mean anything I'm thinking?

Ms. S: Yep. Like I bet if we could have gotten into Louis's head, we might have heard him thinking something like, "I can't stand this. Wilson is a real creep. I have to shut him up. Nobody can laugh at me," things like that.

Randall: I bet he was thinking other things too (smiling), but we shouldn't say that stuff.

Reflection "in" Practice

Randall appears to be following along with the idea of self-talk, mediating feelings, and actions. If you reflect on his last comment, is there anything that seems to call out for your response? As a counselor with a cognitive orientation, you would want to help Randall identify all his thoughts about those events associated with his outbursts.

As Ms. Schulman listens to Randall's response, she is a bit concerned that he may feel as if he needs to edit his thoughts when keeping his log. She wants to be sure that he knows it is okay to write down anything and everything that he is thinking. She thinks, "I don't want him editing his thoughts before we get a chance to analyze and debate them."

Ms. S: You may be right about that. But you know what? Since it's just you and me who are going to read what you write, it's okay to write down anything you are thinking. In fact, the more thoughts you can "hear" and the more you write down, the better it will be. So, don't feel like you should make it all nice for me. We will be the only ones to see what you write. Okay?

Randall: I'll try. I'm pitching this Saturday, so maybe that would be a good day to write about.

Ms. S: That would be good. But really, any time you find that you are getting angry, even just a little, that would be a good time to write down all the things we talked about in these three columns. You know, describe the event, then how you are feeling and acting and most importantly—right here in the middle—everything that you are saying to yourself at that moment. Okay?

(Continued)

(Continued)

Randall: Okay.

Ms. S: Randall, I am really impressed by how much you are participating in this with me. You really are getting it, and I think it's really going to help. So thank you.

Randall: This is fun (smiling).

Ms. S: I'm glad you like it. So, how about if you get back to class and I'll see you on Monday, and we'll see how the weekend went?

Randall: Okay, see ya.

Ms. S: Hey—good luck at your game!

Reflection "on" Practice

As you reflect on the exchange, what are you feelings about: (1) the nature of the working relationship, (2) Randall's level of understanding and insight, (3) Randall's ability to benefit from a cognitive intervention. As you look forward to the session on Monday, what are your goals and plans?

As Ms. Schulman reflects on her session, she feels very confident that the relationship is strong and truly collaborative. She is impressed by this young student's ability to grasp these concepts and engage in such self-exploration. As she thinks about the upcoming session, she anticipates that Randall may have difficulty doing the homework and she wants to be sure to frame anything he does as valuable data. She wants him to experience success and not see this like other homework that would be graded or something to be passed or failed. As she looks forward to the session on Monday, she sets a tentative goal to take one of the situations he identified and help him elaborate on all his thoughts, not just voluntary thoughts. She is hoping that she will be able to process his automatic thoughts and even begin to demonstrate how to debate and reformulate any faulty thinking.

Session 4: Reviewing the Thought Log and the Use of a Seven-Column Approach

Ms. S: Good morning, Randall. How did your game go on Saturday?

Randall: We won. We're in first place now.

Ms. S: That's super. It sounds like you must have pitched pretty well?

Randall: Not really.

Ms. S: Hmm, well, there I go jumping to conclusions. Would you want to tell me about the game?

Randall: I did okay for the first three innings, striking out four batters and only allowing one hit. But then I hit a batter. I didn't mean to but the ball kind of slipped. After that I kind of lost it. I started walking people and actually walked in a run. I was getting really down on myself.

Ms. S: Down on yourself?

Randall: Yeah. I started freakin' and getting angry so the coach pulled me.

Reflection "in" Practice

As you listen to Randall's presentation of the events, where do you see the opportunity for intervention?

As Ms. Schulman reflects on Randall's comments, she is aware of the need to be supportive, but also is "excited" that perhaps this would be a good example to use in order to demonstrate the thought-feeling connection and the identification of "faulty" thinking. She feels that maybe since Randall is able to openly discuss the event, that he is not too sensitive about it and may be able to see the benefits of challenging that thinking by checking the evidence. She wants to first help him identify the "reality" of the event as opposed to his interpretation.

Ms. S: Sorry to hear that. When you say, "pulled you," do you mean you were out of the game?

Randall: No, I played shortstop.

Ms. S: Oh, so it wasn't like you were so bad that you couldn't play.

Randall: No, I played really good. I had three hits and I even hit a triple.

Ms. S: That's great! Did you write about that?

Randall: Yeah. I'm not sure I did it the right way. Here (pulling out a paper).

Ms. S: Super! Look at this. You did a great job. So, let's see, you have in the "Event" column, "I was pitching and I hit the first batter and then walked some people and was pitching really bad." Yep, that's good. Now, over here, you wrote that you were "feeling angry and yelling at myself and not focusing." This is right on. Great job. This is exactly the kind of data we need.

Randall: I was really a jerk, acting like a baby—mumbling and kicking the dirt on the mound.

Reflection "in" Practice

Randall is certainly engaged in the process. At this point in the interaction, what if any "intervention" might you employ?

(Continued)

(Continued)

   Ms. Schulman is excited about Randall's active participation in the counseling. But hearing his interpretation of his actions as reflective of his "person" concerns Ms. Schulman and she thinks that this is a teachable moment and wants to try a subtle confrontation.

Ms. S: Well, it sounds like you were really upset and angry. And while I may agree with you that mumbling and kicking the mound may look a little silly, I'm not sure that qualifies you for total "jerkhood" or "baby" status (smiling).

Randall: I guess not (smiling).

Ms. S: Okay, let's get back to our example. You were really upset, angry, and mumbling and kicking the dirt. Now, let's see what you were thinking, what you were saying to yourself that was making you so upset (looking at the middle column). Wow. Great job. So you have, "I'm making an ass out of myself. I'm blowing this game. What a loser. I should just quit."

Randall: But that's how it felt. I *was* blowing it.

Ms. S: Well, remember when we say things like this to ourselves, and believe them, we do feel as if they are true, but they may not be. Remember Marconi? He felt his thoughts were true but we know they weren't accurate. Right?

Randall: Right. But boy, it felt real. I really felt like the worst player on the team.

Ms. S: That's sad, because I know those feeling were real. But even though that's how you felt, your thinking that you were the worst player or that you completely blew the game and you were a loser and should never play baseball again, those thoughts weren't accurate. They really weren't what was actually going on.

Randall: But I was blowing it!

Ms. S: Okay, let's check that out. In fact, we have a couple of things we need to check out to see if they are true. Like you believe you are blowing it. Okay, that's one thought we need to check. And then you believe because you are blowing it, it means you should never play again. And finally, because you are blowing it, and therefore you should never play again, that somehow makes you a loser! Whew . . . lots to check out.

Randall: How?

Reflection "in" Practice

What's your "read" on Randall's engagement at this point? Do you feel he is understanding? How do you "check" all of his thinking?

Ms. Schulman feels that Randall's "how" was truly a statement of interest. She thinks this may be the right time to expand on his log and include evidence that supports or does not support his interpretations of the event. But, she reminds herself that she needs to be clear, concrete, and go slowly since this is a difficult process to learn.

Ms. S: How? Okay. You and I are going to become detectives and what we are going to do is take your thought and then we will search for hard, cold "facts," just like in a detective story. You know, facts that prove you were blowing the game! Oh, and facts that you are a loser! But we need to stick to the facts, only real evidence, if we are going to be good detectives.

Randall: Like *CSI?*

Ms. S: Yep. Okay, so, what evidence would you give me that points to you blowing the game and being a loser? Wait . . . wait . . . How about if I draw two more columns on your sheet. And in this one I'll say "Evidence that supports my thinking" and then over here I'll put "Evidence that doesn't support my thinking." Okay . . . so give it to me. What's the evidence? Remember the facts and just the facts (smiling).

Randall: Well, I hit a guy and walked in a run.

Ms. S: Okay, and that's evidence of what?

Randall: I'm blowing it.

Reflection "in" Practice

Randall's reference to CSI, *a police show, suggests that he has a frame of reference for testing "hypotheses" with evidence. He has now presented a statement of what he did and he is using it as evidence for his conclusion that he is blowing the game. How would you confront? Challenge? Create cognitive dissonance at this point?*

Ms. Schulman is pleased that Randall is in his "detective" mode and is thrilled about this data recording. However, she sees his conclusion as something she wants to challenge, and challenge in a way that causes him a little cognitive conflict.

Ms. S: Hmm, really? You mean any time a pitcher hits a batter, that's it . . . it's over. He blew it?

Randall: Well, not really.

Ms. S: Okay. So, the fact that you hit someone is really not evidence that you were blowing the entire game. But you know what? It is evidence of something.

(Continued)

(Continued)

Randall: Yeah.

Ms. S: Well, let's see. If I saw you or anyone else hit a batter, what would that be evidence of?

Randall: I guess it could mean that I lost my concentration or the ball slipped, or my arm was tired.

Ms. S: That's great. Are any of those "true"?

Randall: Yeah. I was trying to throw a curve and the ball kind of slipped.

Ms. S: That's fantastic. You know, I am going to write that down over here as evidence not supporting my belief I'm blowing it, I'm a loser, and I should quit. I will write down, "The ball slipped as I was trying to throw a curve ball." Anything else?

Randall: Yeah. My arm was getting tired and I really think I wasn't focusing.

Ms. S: Okay, but these things are also *not* evidence that you blew the game and were a loser and should quit, 'cause if they were . . . ?

Randall: When it happened to other pitchers they would have to quit?

Ms. S: Randall, you are really a good detective (smiling). Okay. I'll write that down in the column over here as evidence not supporting your belief, hmm, "My arm is tired and I'm losing concentration. I'm starting to pitch poorly." Does that sound accurate?

Randall: Yeah, that was true.

Ms. S: Okay, so what other evidence do you have to support your thinking that you were a loser, blowing it, and should quit?

Randall: Well, the coach pulled me.

Ms. S: Pulled you?

Randall: Well he pulled me from pitching and put me in at shortstop.

Ms. S: Okay. The fact that the coach changed your position—does that support the idea that you blew the game and you are a loser and you should quit, or does it maybe mean something else?

Randall: I guess it means I was blowing it as a pitcher but not being a complete loser.

Ms. S: Randall, that's fantastic. That sounds right on to me, because if you were a complete loser and should never ever play baseball, I guess the coach would have told you to hit the road and run away (smiling).

Randall: Yeah, and I did a really good job at short, I had three hits and I even started a double play.

Ms. S: Okay, so let me write that down as evidence that doesn't support the idea you are a loser and blowing it and should quit. So let's put that here, "I went three for four and hit a triple and started a double play." Okay?

Randall: Yeah, and actually, my triple drove in two runs and they were the winning runs.

Ms. S: Wow . . . that certainly doesn't sound like a guy who blew that game and should quit baseball forever . . . a real loser. I'll put that in this "Nonsupport" column, "Drove in the winning runs."

Reflection "in" Practice

It appears Randall is starting to make some fine line distinctions between a tired arm or loss of concentration as opposed to the more general state-ment of blowing everything and then the personalization of that statement to reflect his value as a "loser." What do you feel needs to happen now? Where would you go and how would you get there?

Ms. Schulman is really impressed with Randall's ability to follow the process and engage in it, offering additional data to support or fail to support his initial thoughts. She wants to highlight the value of this debating process, in terms of helping him not only rework his thinking about this issue so that the thoughts more accurately reflect the reality, but also the more general value of this as a style of approach to all future situations in which he finds himself unduly upset and angry.

Ms. S: Wow! I'm impressed. I'm impressed that you turned a double play and hit in the winning run, but truthfully I'm more impressed that you just argued with your silly thinking!

Randall: Huh?

Ms. S: Well, look (writing down in the columns of "Evidence" and "Nonevidence"). See, here we'll write down, "Pulled as a pitcher" and over here, we'll write down, "Played shortstop and started a double play." That's what you just pointed out and it doesn't seem to fit the conclusion that you blew the game and that you are a loser and you should quit. So Randall, if we only use this one column of information, you know, "I hit a player, walked in run, pulled as pitcher," I might think that you didn't do so well, but if we include *all* the data, you know, went three for four, hit a triple, started a double play at short. What do you think I would conclude about the way you played?

Randall: I guess I would think, "I did well for three innings but then lost my concentration pitching, but was still able to play good defense and hit."

(Continued)

(Continued)

Ms. S: Fantastic! And if that is what you were thinking, rather than, "I blew it. I'm a loser. I should quit," how do you think you would feel?

Randall: I think I would feel pretty good about the game and how I played, but I still would be frustrated that I lost my concentration and didn't pitch as well as I wanted.

Ms. S: Randall, you are right on. And, I bet with that frustration you would try harder next time to stay focused.

Randall: Yeah.

Ms. S: Wow. If only we could have climbed into your head and argued with you when you were thinking you were a loser and should quit and helped you look at *all* the evidence, I bet you may have been able to regain your focus or at least you wouldn't have felt as bad as you did. I bet even if you were disappointed with your pitching, you wouldn't have felt as bad as you did and wouldn't have acted the way you did.

Randall: Yeah, but how do I do that? It's too late. The game is over!

Reflection "in" Practice

Randall seems to be really getting the idea. How do you respond to his last comment implying that this is a good idea but too late?

With Randall right about the game being over, Ms. Schulman feels that this is a great opportunity to get him to understand that correcting our thinking about old events helps to develop a new way of approaching similar situations in the future.

Ms. S: Well, that game is over, but our silly thinking can come up in others situations and cause us problems. But the cool thing is that we can start to correct that silly thinking and each time we argue with ourselves, even when it is way after the event is over, it helps to reduce the chance that we will use that silly thinking in the future. If you just keep practicing what you and I just did, you will develop the habit to use straight thinking rather than silly thoughts. It just requires you to keep practicing describing the situations, listening to your thinking, and then looking for evidence that supports or fails to support that thinking, and then use all the evidence to "rethink" the situation. Whew. I know that sounds like a lot, but with practice, it gets much easier, almost automatic!

Randall: Sounds like a lot of work.

Ms. S:	It is. But the more you do it, the easier and more automatic it becomes, like any new skill you may be working on. Are you trying anything new that seems really hard but is getting easier with practice?
Randall:	Yeah. My dad has been teaching me golf and boy that's got tons of things you have to remember . . . but I'm getting better.
Ms. S:	Once again, you are right on! Learning a new skill or approach takes practice, but it does get easier and I bet the payoff, like hitting a good drive, makes all the work worthwhile?
Randall:	Yeah.
Ms. S:	And the same is true when you start to see that you are not getting so angry or losing your cool. You will see that it is really worth the effort.
Randall:	Yeah, I could stay in the game (smiling).
Ms. S:	Yep, and stay out of Dr. Kim's office (smiling).
Randall:	Yep (smiling).

Reflection "in" Practice

As the session draws to a close, what homework, if any, might you assign?

Ms. Schulman believes that Randall really has a super grasp on the concept and the process, and wants to encourage him to employ it on his own.

Ms. S:	Would you be willing to give this seven-column approach a try? I bet if you would write out and debate a couple of situations and then "rewrite" your thinking so that it includes all the evidence, I bet you will find that even as an event is happening, you will start to rethink what it means. But it will take a little practice. Are you up for it?
Randall:	I could try.
Ms. S:	How about if you give it a try for the remainder of this week. And on Monday, I will check in with you to see how you are doing, and if you have any questions, I can answer them on Monday. Okay?
Randall:	Okay.

Reflection "on" Practice

What are your expectations for your meeting with Randall on Monday, and what would your goals be for the next phase of this counseling?

(Continued)

(Continued)

Ms. Schulman believes Randall has really latched onto the cognitive model and she's hoping he will be able to successfully practice on his own. As she thinks about the upcoming meeting, she has two plans. First, if he had difficulty, she will help him work through the examples he may have and then set up another three- or four-day practice period. But if he shows evidence of really understanding and employing the process, she wants to separate so that he can generalize what he does in the counseling office to his day-to-day experience.

Session 5: Brief Check-In

Ms. S: Randall, super job (looking at his journal). You really have done an excellent job with the debating.

Randall: It was fun (smiling). I was even able to teach my dad.

Ms. S: Teach your dad?

Randall: Yeah. He was out fixing the lawn mower, and I was helping, and he broke the carburetor and skinned his knuckles and kind of went ballistic. I won't say what he said. But when he calmed down, he apologized for his language and I said that it's a shame that he gave the lawn mower so much power (smiling).

Ms. S: You did? What did he say?

Randall: He sounded like me. He said, "Power? What are talking about?" And it was cool. I told him what you and me have been talking about, all that thinking stuff. I'm not sure I got all of it correct but it was fun telling him. My dad really thought it was cool and he reminded me that he told me that's what he meant when he told me that I should just keep saying, "Relax, stay focused."

Ms. S: Randall, keep that up and you will be taking my job (smiling)!

Reflection "in" Practice

How do you interpret this event and what does it lead you to conclude in terms of your next step? In particular, what, if anything, might you want to highlight and reinforce?

Ms. Schulman realizes that the fact that Randall's dad went "ballistic" may be something to highlight. It helps point out that we all have overreactions to events as a result of our distorting thinking, but she also sees the need to point out that we can stop that with practice.

Ms. S: You know, I'm sorry your dad had a problem with the lawn mower, but it just kind of shows us that we all can take a simple situation and misinterpret it and make it a catastrophe! I bet if your dad knew how to do the seven-column approach, he could learn to keep things in focus, just like you are doing.

Randall: I showed him my notes and he said he was going to try it, especially at work. He told me that he knows he lets things get to him and he really wants that to stop.

Ms. S: That's great. See, you are not only helping yourself but you really are helping your dad.

Randall: Yeah (smiling).

Reflection "in" Practice

It seems that Randall is not only buying into the model, but has a natural ally in his dad. As you come to the end of this session, what are your immediate goals and plans for future support?

   Ms. Schulman believes that Randall really has a super grasp on the concept and the process, and in line with her presession reflections "on" practice, she decides to encourage him to employ the technique on his own. She hopes that having Randall engage in this process on his own might help not only strengthen this way of thinking, but also help him generalize outside of the counselor's office. She wants to "push" him a little to do the work on his own.

Ms. S: I have an idea. Since you are really doing a fantastic job with this, why not try it on your own for the next week or so. Maybe you could send me some examples to my e-mail and I could maybe help you rethink the situation? I could be like your coach.

Randall: Yeah. I'd like to try it and my dad can coach me too. But would it be okay if I stop down if I have a question?

Ms. S: Of course, if you have a question or something comes up that you want to talk about, you know I'm here, so stop down. But I really would like you to shoot me a couple of e-mail examples that you are working through. Okay?

Randall: Yeah, I can do that.

Ms. S: Okay. I think this will be neat. We'll let you practice a little on your own and then we will get together and decide what's next. Okay?

(Continued)

(Continued)

Randall: Yeah. Okay.

Ms. S: Great. Now get out there and check all the evidence before drawing conclusions, and I'll see you in a week or so.

Reflection "in" Practice

At this point in the interaction, how comfortable are you with sending Randall out on his own? Ms. Schulman is using the e-mail as a way of maintaining contact. What, if anything, might you do in the time between contacts?

Ms. Schulman wants to give Randall the space to take ownership and responsibility for debating his thinking, but appreciating he is still a young student, she wants to make herself a little more available for support. As such, she thinks that she will try to "accidentally" run into Randall at lunch early next week just to let him know that she is still thinking of him. Further, she thinks that she may send him an e-mail simply asking, "How's it going?" as a way of stimulating his practice.

E-mail Contact

Over the course of the next four days, Ms. Schulman e-mails Randall reminders about drawing conclusions without the evidence and the need to check "thinking," especially at times when he is feeling angry. Randall reports that he is doing better and not getting in trouble in school (a point validated by his teachers) and he provides Ms. Schulman with a couple of situations where he was able to use the seven-column approach and reformulate his thinking. However, prior to the scheduled session, Randall is sent to in-school detention for verbally attacking a classmate during science class.

Reflection "on" Practice

As you plan to meet with Randall, what special concerns might you have and what would your goals for the upcoming session be?

Ms. Schulman, while seeing the issue of the science class as just an example of "jumping track," is concerned that Randall will be defensive and down on himself. She wants to be sure to affirm all the good work he has been doing and the material he sent via e-mail. So, while not making light of the event, she wants to be sure to approach it as a "matter of fact" and emphasize the reality that old habits are hard to break. She wants to give him the message that he just needs to keep practicing. She also wants to highlight that there will be times when he jumps track, since none of us are perfect, but when we jump track we just need to get back on a straight way of thinking.

Session 6: Resistance

Ms. S: Really, I'm impressed by how well you were doing. Using that seven-column form is not that easy and yet the examples you sent me were right on. You really did a super job arguing with yourself and correcting any silly thinking.

Randall: I was doing okay, until yesterday.

Ms. S: You were doing better than okay; you were doing really well. Your teachers were really impressed by how much you were cooperating and engaging with the other students and seemed to be really in control and relaxed. I know yesterday was a rough spot. What happened?

Randall: We were working in pairs in science lab and Ronald was my partner. Well, he kept goofing up and wasn't doing his share of the work. I kept saying really nicely, "come on Ronald let's do this," and things like that, but he kept screwing around. Well, at one point, he knocked the scale over and it made a loud noise and Mrs. Morton yelled at us. She said, "Randall and Ronald, see me after class. You guys have to grow up and do your work." I don't know. I just freaked and started yelling at Ronald, calling him an ass, a real jerk, and then I got angry at Mrs. Morton, telling her she's unfair and I didn't care about her dumb experiment. So I got an in-house suspension.

Ms. S: Maybe we could look at this and see if there was evidence that would lead to some other thoughts and actions? Like Mrs. Morton yelled at both of you, rather than just Ronald. When she did that, do you remember what you were thinking?

Randall: I was thinking she's unfair. She's always blaming me. I wasn't doing anything wrong, but I always get blamed. This was unfair.

Ms. S: Okay. So, the actual facts were that she corrected both of you and you are saying that she is also, *always*, unfairly blaming you for things that are not your fault. Wow. If that was true, I guess I could understand how frustrating that would be. But does she *always* blame you?

Randall: No (smiling). In fact, she's told me that I have a scientist mind . . . so I guess she likes me.

Ms. S: Okay, that's better, a little more information. But how do we make sense out of these pieces of information? First, she likes you, but here she is correcting you and not just Ronald?

Randall: Well, she wasn't watching us, so she didn't know who did what, and I guess since we are partners she just yelled at both of us.

(Continued)

(Continued)

Ms. S: Fantastic. You really do have a good scientist mind, looking for evidence and then reforming your silly thoughts. So, the evidence seems to suggest not that she is always treating you unfairly, but that she probably did not know who did what, and yet knew it was coming from your area so she just nabbed both of you. So, I wonder how you would feel and maybe what you would have done if when she said, "Randall and Ronald knock it off. See me after school," you thought, "Oh, boy. She didn't see it was Ronald screwing around and that I was doing all the work."

Randall: I don't know. I still would be frustrated that she had me coming back after school.

Ms. S: Frustrated, yep...that makes sense. But it doesn't sound like you would have flipped out?

Randall: Probably not. I probably would have said something to Ronald like, "Way to go, jerk," but then I probably would have shown Mrs. Morton that I was doing all the work. I like her and wouldn't want her to think I was screwing around.

Ms. S: So, thinking she probably didn't see what happened would result in you feeling some frustration, but not anger and that would be useful because you would explain to her what really happened.

Randall: Yeah, I guess.

Ms. S: But I'm wondering which thought is accurate, you know, which way of thinking has the evidence to support it. Is it true she always blames you, that she is always unfair? Or is there more evidence that she wasn't sure of who was doing what and simply punished the pair?

Randall: I can see that she wasn't watching us and it wasn't that she was being unfair and picking on me. I can see that now, but not then. This is really hard. I don't know if I can do this.

Reflection "in" Practice

It is clear Randall understands, but is also frustrated that he hasn't perfected the process. What, if anything, would you do at this point?

Ms. Schulman wants to be sure that Randall isn't allowed to believe he "can't get this," but rather reform that thought so that it does reflect the difficulty with changing our thinking, and the need to accept that sometimes we will be less than perfect.

Ms. S: Yep. It is hard. But look here (pointing to log), you already did it . . . you *do* get it. You just did it here with me as we rethought the situation with Ms. Morton and look, you did it two other times (looking at Randall's log). Look here, the situation with your brother and over here at Sunday's game. So, it is hard, and you won't be perfect at it but the more you practice the better you'll get!

Randall: I guess.

Ms. S: I bet that when you learned how to throw a curve ball that that wasn't easy, and probably you still don't do it perfectly every time but . . .

Randall: You got that right (interrupting). I hung one on Sunday and the kid nailed it over the fence for a homerun!

Ms. S: Yeah, but look, you didn't get down or lose focus. In fact, you wrote here that you struck the next batter out with a curve ball. So if this is correct, it looks like you said to yourself, "Ouch. I hung that out. I have to follow through when I throw a curve," and that thought helped you get back into the game and do it correctly. See, you are using good thinking and learning to argue with your silly thoughts. It gets easier with practice, just like throwing a curve (smiling).

Randall: It's still frustrating when I flip out.

Ms. S: I'm sure it is, and it seems you could interpret that a couple of different ways. What do you think? When you flip out, what could you say to yourself about that? What does that mean?

Randall: I guess I could say, "I'll never get it" or as you said, "It's hard and I have to keep practicing."

Ms. S: That's super. And I bet that thinking, "I'll never get this," would probably result in you quitting and then you'd be right. You wouldn't get it. But, thinking, "This is hard and I have to keep practicing" will probably do what?

Randall: Get me to practice?

Ms. S: Right on.

Reflection "in" Practice

Randall is certainly an insightful child. While he might be an interesting student to continue to work with, the reality is that this counselor and all school counselors have much to do. So where would you like to go with Randall at this point in the counseling? How might you respond at this point to get there?

(Continued)

(Continued)

Ms. Schulman wants to affirm all that Randall has done and encourage him to keep practicing. While she knows there will be setbacks, she wants him to recognize that while she is here for him, he can also rely on himself by using the journaling and looking at the evidence, two things that he has already employed and that have helped.

Ms. S: You are really getting to be a "cognitive dude" (smiling), taking the power back.

Randall: Thanks (smiling).

Ms. S: Look, I'm thinking that since there is a lot of stuff coming up in the next few weeks, you know, baseball and exams and things like that, and we both will have lots to do, why don't we take a small break from meeting and you continue to use your journal and look for evidence to practice attacking silly thinking, and even e-mailing me on how you are doing. What do you think about that plan?

Randall: That would be okay.

Ms. S: Now, I don't want you getting *too* crazy about your journaling, but I really would like you to try to do one or two situations a week as practice.

Randall: But what if nothing comes up?

Ms. S: Well, that would be great. But even if nothing comes up, I bet you could remember one or two old situations where you lost it and you could practice with those. Remember, we are not just trying to help with this or that situation, but trying to help you learn a new way of thinking about all events so even practicing on old events can help develop that ability.

Randall: My dad tells me to do that for pitching. He'll tell me to remember how I pitched to different batters and in my mind rethink what I did and what I could do differently. He says it will help me the next time.

Ms. S: Same thing! Boy, you really do get this. Now remember, you can send me an e-mail or stop down if something comes up and what I'll do is track you down in a couple of weeks to see how it's going. Okay?

Randall: That's cool.

Postscript

Over the next two weeks, Ms. Schulman made sure that she caught Randall in the hallways and at lunch just to "check in." Randall's teachers reported that his behavior had significantly improved and that even when showing some frustration and irritation he was able to control his anger, calm down rapidly, and apologize without a request to do so.

Ms. Schulman did not continue the "formal" contract for counseling. She felt that the sessions were beneficial; a point supported by the teachers' observations. She felt good that Randall's e-mails gave evidence that he understood the connection of thinking to feelings and that he even developed the ability to debate and reformulate his thinking so that it more accurately reflected the "evidence."

Reflection "on" Practice

Ms. Schulman has chosen to "end" the formal contact with Randall at this point in time and place in the counseling relationship. What would you have done differently? As you reflect on this practice what, if anything, would you do next?

As Ms. Schulman reflects on her interaction with Randall, she feels good about herself, the direction of the interaction, and the outcome. She really enjoyed working with Randall and while believing he understands and can apply the principles she introduced, she questions if he'll keep journaling and practicing. To that end, she decides to research existing curriculum and packaged materials that could be employed to develop a guidance unit to provide to all sixth graders. She feels that maybe introducing a tagline or slogan like "take the power back'" might help the students remind each other to challenge their silly thoughts throughout the year.

Epilogue

A Beginning . . . Not an End

While we have come to the end of this book, it is hopefully only the beginning of your own ongoing development as a reflective school counselor. The material presented in this book has provided you with an introduction to the world of a cognitive-oriented school counselor, and the procedural thinking that guides his or her practice. However, it is truly just the beginning.

As school counselors, we know the value of maintaining competence in the skills we use and we know the ethical mandate to continue to develop those skills (See Resource, Standard E.1.c). While being open to new procedures demonstrated to be effective for the diverse population with whom we work, we must also recognize the limitations of our professional competence to use these procedures (See Resource, Standard E.1.a). The material provided in this book is but a first step to developing that competency.

Becoming an expert in counseling, as is true of any profession, requires continued training, personal reflection, and supervision. It is hoped that with this introduction to the theory and practice of a cognitive-oriented counselor, you will be stimulated to continue in that training, personal reflection, and supervision and as a result grow in thinking and acting like an expert.

Resource

Ethical Standards for School Counselors

The American School Counselor Association's (ASCA) Ethical Standards for School Counselors were adopted by the ASCA Delegate Assembly, March 19,1984, revised March 27, 1992, June 25, 1998 and June 26, 2004. For a PDF version of the Ethical Standards visit www.schoolcounselor.org/content.asp?contentid=173.

PREAMBLE

The American School Counselor Association (ASCA) is a professional organization whose members are certified/licensed in school counseling with unique qualifications and skills to address the academic, personal/ social, and career development needs of all students. Professional school counselors are advocates, leaders, collaborators, and consultants who create opportunities for equity in access and success in educational opportunities by connecting their programs to the mission of schools and subscribing to the following tenets of professional responsibility:

- Each person has the right to be respected, be treated with dignity, and have access to a comprehensive school counseling program that advocates for and affirms all students from diverse populations regardless of ethnic/racial status, age, economic status, special needs, English as a second language or other language group, immigration status, sexual orientation, gender, gender identity/expression, family type, religious/spiritual identity, and appearance.
- Each person has the right to receive the information and support needed to move toward self-direction and self-development and affirmation within one's group identities, with special care being

given to students who have historically not received adequate educational services: students of color, low socioeconomic students, students with disabilities and students with nondominant language backgrounds.

- Each person has the right to understand the full magnitude and meaning of his or her educational choices and how those choices will affect future opportunities.
- Each person has the right to privacy and thereby the right to expect the counselor-student relationship to comply with all laws, policies, and ethical standards pertaining to confidentiality in the school setting.

In this document, ASCA specifies the principles of ethical behavior necessary to maintain the high standards of integrity, leadership, and professionalism among its members. The Ethical Standards for School Counselors were developed to clarify the nature of ethical responsibilities held in common by school counseling professionals. The purposes of this document are to:

- Serve as a guide for the ethical practices of all professional school counselors regardless of level, area, population served or membership in this professional association.
- Provide self-appraisal and peer evaluations regarding counselor responsibilities to students, parents/guardians, colleagues, and professional associates, schools, communities, and the counseling profession.
- Inform those served by the school counselor of acceptable counselor practices and expected professional behavior.

A.1. Responsibilities to Students

The professional school counselor:

a. Has a primary obligation to the student, who is to be treated with respect as a unique individual.

b. Is concerned with the educational, academic, career, personal, and social needs and encourages the maximum development of every student.

c. Respects the student's values and beliefs and does not impose the counselor's personal values.

d. Is knowledgeable of laws, regulations, and policies relating to students and strives to protect and inform students regarding their rights.

A.2. Confidentiality

The professional school counselor:

a. Informs students of the purposes, goals, techniques, and rules of procedure under which they may receive counseling at or before the time when the counseling relationship is entered. Disclosure notice includes the limits of confidentiality such as the possible necessity for consulting with other professionals, privileged communication, and legal or authoritative restraints. The meaning and limits of confidentiality are defined in developmentally appropriate terms to students.

b. Keeps information confidential unless disclosure is required to prevent clear and imminent danger to the student or others or when legal requirements demand that confidential information be revealed. Counselors will consult with appropriate professionals when in doubt as to the validity of an exception.

c. In absence of state legislation expressly forbidding disclosure, considers the ethical responsibility to provide information to an identified third party who, by his or her relationship with the student, is at a high risk of contracting a disease that is commonly known to be communicable and fatal. Disclosure requires satisfaction of all of the following conditions:

   • Student identifies partner or the partner is highly identifiable.
   • Counselor recommends the student notify partner and refrain from further high-risk behavior.
   • Student refuses.
   • Counselor informs the student of the intent to notify the partner.
   • Counselor seeks legal consultation as to the legalities of informing the partner.

d. Requests of the court that disclosure not be required when the release of confidential information may potentially harm a student or the counseling relationship.

e. Protects the confidentiality of students' records and releases personal data in accordance with prescribed laws and school policies. Student information stored and transmitted electronically is treated with the same care as traditional student records.

f. Protects the confidentiality of information received in the counseling relationship as specified by federal and state laws, written policies, and applicable ethical standards. Such information is only to be revealed to others with the informed consent of the student, consistent with the counselor's ethical obligation.

g. Recognizes his or her primary obligation for confidentiality is to the student but balances that obligation with an understanding of the legal and inherent rights of parents/guardians to be the guiding voice in their children's lives.

A.3. Counseling Plans

The professional school counselor:

a. Provides students with a comprehensive school counseling program that includes a strong emphasis on working jointly with all students to develop academic and career goals.

b. Advocates for counseling plans supporting students' right to choose from the wide array of options when they leave secondary education. Such plans will be regularly reviewed to update students regarding critical information they need to make informed decisions.

A.4. Dual Relationships

The professional school counselor:

a. Avoids dual relationships that might impair his or her objectivity and increase the risk of harm to the student (e.g., counseling one's family members, close friends, or associates). If a dual relationship is unavoidable, the counselor is responsible for taking action to eliminate or reduce the potential for harm. Such safeguards might include informed consent, consultation, supervision, and documentation.

b. Avoids dual relationships with school personnel that might infringe on the integrity of the counselor/student relationship.

A.5. Appropriate Referrals

The professional school counselor:

a. Makes referrals when necessary or appropriate to outside resources. Appropriate referrals may necessitate informing both parents/guardians and students of applicable resources and making proper plans for transitions with minimal interruption of services. Students retain the right to discontinue the counseling relationship at any time.

A.6. Group Work

The professional school counselor:

a. Screens prospective group members and maintains an awareness of participants' needs and goals in relation to the goals of the group. The counselor takes reasonable precautions to protect members from physical and psychological harm resulting from interaction within the group.

b. Notifies parents/guardians and staff of group participation if the counselor deems it appropriate and if consistent with school board policy or practice.

c. Establishes clear expectations in the group setting and clearly states that confidentiality in group counseling cannot be guaranteed. Given the developmental and chronological ages of minors in schools, the counselor recognizes the tenuous nature of confidentiality for minors renders some topics inappropriate for group work in a school setting.

d. Follows up with group members and documents proceedings as appropriate.

A.7. Danger to Self or Others

The professional school counselor:

a. Informs parents/guardians or appropriate authorities when the student's condition indicates a clear and imminent danger to the student or others. This is to be done after careful deliberation and, where possible, after consultation with other counseling professionals.

b. Will attempt to minimize threat to a student and may choose to (1) inform the student of actions to be taken, (2) involve the student in a three-way communication with parents/guardians when breaching confidentiality, or (3) allow the student to have input as to how and to whom the breach will be made.

A.8. Student Records

The professional school counselor:

a. Maintains and secures records necessary for rendering professional services to the student as required by laws, regulations, institutional procedures, and confidentiality guidelines.

b. Keeps sole-possession records separate from students' educational records in keeping with state laws.

c. Recognizes the limits of sole-possession records and understands these records are a memory aid for the creator and in absence of privilege communication may be subpoenaed and may become educational records when they (1) are shared with others in verbal or written form, (2) include information other than professional opinion or personal observations, and/or (3) are made accessible to others.

d. Establishes a reasonable timeline for purging sole-possession records or case notes. Suggested guidelines include shredding sole-possession records when the student transitions to the next level, transfers to another school, or graduates. Careful discretion and deliberation should be applied before destroying sole-possession records that may be needed by a court of law such as notes on child abuse, suicide, sexual harassment, or violence.

A.9. Evaluation, Assessment, and Interpretation

The professional school counselor:

a. Adheres to all professional standards regarding selecting, administering, and interpreting assessment measures and only utilizes assessment measures that are within the scope of practice for school counselors.

b. Seeks specialized training regarding the use of electronically-based testing programs in administering, scoring, and interpreting that may differ from that required in more traditional assessments.

c. Considers confidentiality issues when utilizing evaluative or assessment instruments and electronically-based programs.

d. Provides interpretation of the nature, purposes, results, and potential impact of assessment/evaluation measures in language the student(s) can understand.

e. Monitors the use of assessment results and interpretations, and takes reasonable steps to prevent others from misusing the information.

f. Uses caution when utilizing assessment techniques, making evaluations, and interpreting the performance of populations not represented in the norm group on which an instrument is standardized.

g. Assesses the effectiveness of his or her program in having an impact on students' academic, career, and personal/social development through accountability measures especially examining efforts to close achievement, opportunity, and attainment gaps.

A.10. Technology

The professional school counselor:

a. Promotes the benefits of and clarifies the limitations of various appropriate technological applications. The counselor promotes technological applications (1) that are appropriate for the student's individual needs, (2) that the student understands how to use and (3) for which follow-up counseling assistance is provided.

b. Advocates for equal access to technology for all students, especially those historically underserved.

c. Takes appropriate and reasonable measures for maintaining confidentiality of student information and educational records stored or transmitted over electronic media including although not limited to fax, electronic mail, and instant messaging.

d. While working with students on a computer or similar technology, takes reasonable and appropriate measures to protect students from objectionable and/or harmful online material.

e. Who is engaged in the delivery of services involving technologies such as the telephone, videoconferencing, and the Internet takes responsible steps to protect students and others from harm.

A.11. Student Peer Support Program

The professional school counselor:

Has unique responsibilities when working with student-assistance programs. The school counselor is responsible for the welfare of students participating in peer-to-peer programs under his or her direction.

B. RESPONSIBILITIES TO PARENTS/GUARDIANS

B.1. Parent Rights and Responsibilities

The professional school counselor:

a. Respects the rights and responsibilities of parents/guardians for their children and endeavors to establish, as appropriate, a collaborative relationship with parents/guardians to facilitate the student's maximum development.

b. Adheres to laws, local guidelines, and ethical standards of practice when assisting parents/guardians experiencing family difficulties that interfere with the student's effectiveness and welfare.

c. Respects the confidentiality of parents/guardians.

d. Is sensitive to diversity among families and recognizes that all parents/guardians, custodial and noncustodial, are vested with certain rights and responsibilities for the welfare of their children by virtue of their role and according to law.

B.2. Parents/Guardians and Confidentiality

The professional school counselor:

a. Informs parents/guardians of the counselor's role with emphasis on the confidential nature of the counseling relationship between the counselor and student.

b. Recognizes that working with minors in a school setting may require counselors to collaborate with students' parents/guardians.

c. Provides parents/guardians with accurate, comprehensive, and relevant information in an objective and caring manner, as is appropriate and consistent with ethical responsibilities to the student.

d. Makes reasonable efforts to honor the wishes of parents/guardians concerning information regarding the student, and in cases of divorce or separation exercises a good-faith effort to keep both parents informed with regard to critical information with the exception of a court order.

C. RESPONSIBILITIES TO COLLEAGUES AND PROFESSIONAL ASSOCIATES

C.1. Professional Relationships

The professional school counselor:

a. Establishes and maintains professional relationships with faculty, staff, and administration to facilitate an optimum counseling program.

b. Treats colleagues with professional respect, courtesy, and fairness. The qualifications, views, and findings of colleagues are represented to accurately reflect the image of competent professionals.

c. Is aware of and utilizes related professionals, organizations, and other resources to whom the student may be referred.

C.2. Sharing Information With Other Professionals

The professional school counselor:

a. Promotes awareness and adherence to appropriate guidelines regarding confidentiality, the distinction between public and private information and staff consultation.

b. Provides professional personnel with accurate, objective, concise, and meaningful data necessary to adequately evaluate, counsel, and assist the student.

c. If a student is receiving services from another counselor or other mental health professional, the counselor, with student and/or parent/guardian consent, will inform the other professional and develop clear agreements to avoid confusion and conflict for the student.

d. Is knowledgeable about release of information and parental rights in sharing information.

D. RESPONSIBILITIES TO THE SCHOOL AND COMMUNITY

D.1. Responsibilities to the School

The professional school counselor:

a. Supports and protects the educational program against any infringement not in student's best interest.

b. Informs appropriate officials in accordance with school policy of conditions that may be potentially disruptive or damaging to the school's mission, personnel, and property while honoring the confidentiality between the student and counselor.

c. Is knowledgeable and supportive of the school's mission and connects his or her program to the school's mission.

d. Delineates and promotes the counselor's role and function in meeting the needs of those served. Counselors will notify appropriate officials of conditions that may limit or curtail their effectiveness in providing programs and services.

e. Accepts employment only for positions for which he or she is qualified by education, training, supervised experience, state and national professional credentials, and appropriate professional experience.

f. Advocates that administrators hire only qualified and competent individuals for professional counseling positions.

g. Assists in developing: (1) curricular and environmental conditions appropriate for the school and community, (2) educational procedures and programs to meet students' developmental needs and (3) a systematic evaluation process for comprehensive, developmental, standards-based school counseling programs, services, and personnel. The counselor is guided by the findings of the evaluation data in planning programs and services.

D.2. Responsibility to the Community

The professional school counselor:

a. Collaborates with agencies, organizations and individuals in the community in the best interest of students and without regard to personal reward or remuneration.

b. Extends his or her influence and opportunity to deliver a comprehensive school counseling program to all students by collaborating with community resources for student success.

E. RESPONSIBILITIES TO SELF

E.1. Professional Competence

The professional school counselor:

a. Functions within the boundaries of individual professional competence and accepts responsibility for the consequences of his or her actions.

b. Monitors personal well-being and effectiveness and does not participate in any activity that may lead to inadequate professional services or harm to a student.

c. Strives through personal initiative to maintain professional competence including technological literacy and to keep abreast of professional information. Professional and personal growth are ongoing throughout the counselor's career.

E.2. Diversity

The professional school counselor:

a. Affirms the diversity of students, staff, and families.

b. Expands and develops awareness of his or her own attitudes and beliefs affecting cultural values and biases and strives to attain cultural competence.

c. Possesses knowledge and understanding about how oppression, racism, discrimination, and stereotyping affects her or him personally and professionally.

d. Acquires educational, consultation, and training experiences to improve awareness, knowledge, skills, and effectiveness in working with diverse populations: ethnic/racial status, age, economic status, special needs, ESL or ELL, immigration status, sexual orientation, gender, gender identity/expression, family type, religious/spiritual identity, and appearance.

F. RESPONSIBILITIES TO THE PROFESSION

F.1. Professionalism

The professional school counselor:

a. Accepts the policies and procedures for handling ethical violations as a result of maintaining membership in the American School Counselor Association.

b. Conducts herself or himself in such a manner as to advance individual ethical practice and the profession.

c. Conducts appropriate research and report findings in a manner consistent with acceptable educational and psychological research practices. The counselor advocates for the protection of the individual student's identity when using data for research or program planning.

d. Adheres to ethical standards of the profession, other official policy statements, such as ASCA's position statements, role statement, and the ASCA National Model, and relevant statutes established by federal, state and local governments, and when these are in conflict works responsibly for change.

e. Clearly distinguishes between statements and actions made as a private individual and those made as a representative of the school counseling profession.

f. Does not use his or her professional position to recruit or gain clients, consultees for his or her private practice or to seek and receive unjustified personal gains, unfair advantage, inappropriate relationships, or unearned goods or services.

F.2. Contribution to the Profession

The professional school counselor:

a. Actively participates in local, state, and national associations fostering the development and improvement of school counseling.

b. Contributes to the development of the profession through the sharing of skills, ideas, and expertise with colleagues.

c. Provides support and mentoring to novice professionals.

G. Maintenance of Standards

Ethical behavior among professional school counselors, association members and nonmembers, is expected at all times. When there exists serious doubt as to the ethical behavior of colleagues or if counselors are forced to work in situations or abide by policies that do not reflect the standards as outlined in these Ethical Standards for School Counselors, the counselor is obligated to take appropriate action to rectify the condition. The following procedure may serve as a guide:

1. The counselor should consult confidentially with a professional colleague to discuss the nature of a complaint to see if the professional colleague views the situation as an ethical violation.

2. When feasible, the counselor should directly approach the colleague whose behavior is in question to discuss the complaint and seek resolution.

3. If resolution is not forthcoming at the personal level, the counselor shall utilize the channels established within the school, school district, the state school counseling association, and ASCA's Ethics Committee.

4. If the matter still remains unresolved, referral for review and appropriate action should be made to the Ethics Committees in the following sequence:

   - state school counselor association
   - American School Counselor Association

5. The ASCA Ethics Committee is responsible for:

   - educating and consulting with the membership regarding ethical standards.
   - periodically reviewing and recommending changes in code.
   - receiving and processing questions to clarify the application of such standards; questions must be submitted in writing to the ASCA Ethics chair.
   - handling complaints of alleged violations of the ethical standards. At the national level, complaints should be submitted in writing to the ASCA Ethics Committee, c/o the Executive Director.

SOURCE: American School Counselor Association. Used with permission.

References

Beck, J. S. (1995). *Cognitive therapy: Basics and beyond.* New York: Guilford.

Berg, B. (1990). *The depression management game.* Dayton, OH: Cognitive Counseling Resources.

Burns, D. D. (1999). *The feeling good handbook.* New York: William Morrow and Co.

Chi, M. T. H., Feltovich, P. J., & Glaser, R. (1981). Categorization and representation of physics problems by experts and novices. *Cognitive Science, 5,* 121–152.

Choate-Summers, M. L., Freeman, J. B., Garcia, A. M., Coyne, L., Przeworski, A., & Leonard, H. L. (2008). Clinical considerations when tailoring cognitive behavioral treatment for young children with obsessive compulsive disorder. *Education & Treatment of Children, 31* (3), 395–416.

Dattilio, F. M. (2006). Restructuring schemata from family of origin in couple therapy. *Journal of Cognitive Psychotherapy, 20* (4), 359–373.

Doherr, L., Reynolds, S., Wetherly, J., & Evans, E. H. (2005).Young children's ability to engage in cognitive therapy tasks: Associations with age and educational experience. *Behavioural and Cognitive Psychotherapy, 33* (2), 201–215.

Ellis, A. (2002). Overcoming resistance: A rational emotive behavior therapy integrated approach (2nd ed.) New York: Springer Publishing.

Epictetus. (1955). *Enchiridion.* (G. Long, Trans.). New York: Prometheus Books. (Original work published first century A.D.)

Freeman, A., Pretzer, J., Fleming, B., & Simon, K. (2004). Clinical applications of cognitive therapy (2nd ed.). New York: Kluwer Academic/Plenum Publications.

Friedberg, R. D., & McClure, J. M. (2004). Adolescents. In N. Kazantzis, F. P. Deane, K. R. Ronan, & L. L'Abate (Eds.), *Using homework assignments in cognitive behavior therapy* (pp. 95–116). New York: Routledge/Taylor & Francis Group.

Irving, J. A., & Willliams, D. I. (1995). Critical thinking and reflective practice in counseling. *British Journal of Guidance and Counseling, 23* (1), 107–116.

Kendall, P. C. (1988). *The stop and think workbook.* Philadelphia: Temple University.

Kendall, P. C. (1990). *Coping cat workbook.* Philadelphia: Temple University.

Kendall, P. C., Gosch, E., Furr, J. M., & Sood, E. (2008). Flexibility within fidelity. *Journal of the American Academy of Child & Adolescent Psychiatry, 47* (9), 987–993.

Knell, S. M. (1998). Cognitive-behavioral play therapy. *Journal of Clinical Child Psychology, 27* (1), 28.

Maultsby, Jr., M. C. (1984). *Rational behavior therapy.* Englewood Cliffs, NJ: Prentice-Hall.

Nelson, M. L., & Neufeldt, S. A. (1998). The pedagogy of counseling: A critical examination. *Counselor Education and Supervision, 38,* 70–88.

Pepinsky, H. B., & Pepinsky, P. (1954). *Counseling theory and practice.* New York: Ronald Press.

Piaget, J. (1985). *The equilibration of cognitive structures: The central problem of intellectual development.* Chicago: University of Chicago Press.

Piper, W. (1976). *The little engine that could: The complete original edition.* New York: Platt and Munk.

Prochaska, J. O., & Norcross, J. C. (1994). *Systems of psychotherapy* (3rd ed.). Pacific Grove, CA: Brooks/Cole.

Quakley, S., Coker, S., Palmer, K., & Reynolds, S. (2003). Can children distinguish between thoughts and behaviours? *Behavioural and Cognitive Psychotherapy, 31* (2),159–167.

Quakley, S., Reynolds, S., & Coker, S. (2004). The effect of cues on young children's abilities to discriminate among thoughts, feelings and behaviours. *Behaviour Research and Therapy, 42* (3), 343–356.

Reynolds, S., Girling, E., Coker, S., & Eastwood, L. (2006). The effect of mental health problems on children's ability to discriminate amongst thoughts, feelings and behaviours. *Cognitive Therapy & Research, 30* (5), 599–607.

Stallard, P. (2002). Cognitive behaviour therapy with children and young people: A selective review of key issues. *Behavioural and Cognitive Psychotherapy, 30* (3), 297–309.

Tillett, R. (1996). Psychotherapy assessment and treatment selection. *British Journal of Psychiatry, 168* (1), 10–15.

Vernon, A. (1989). *Thinking, feeling, behaving: An emotional education curriculum for adolescents/Grades 7–12.* Champaign, IL: Research Press.

Index

CORWIN
A SAGE Company

The Corwin logo—a raven striding across an open book—represents the union of courage and learning. Corwin is committed to improving education for all learners by publishing books and other professional development resources for those serving the field of PreK–12 education. By providing practical, hands-on materials, Corwin continues to carry out the promise of its motto: **"Helping Educators Do Their Work Better."**